Careers in Focus

THERAPISTS

SECOND EDITION

Ferguson
An imprint of Infobase Publishing

3 1218 00442 6723

Careers in Focus: Therapists, Second Edition

Copyright © 2008 by Infobase Publishing

Ferguson
An imprint of Infobase Publishing
132 West 31st Street
New York NY 10001

Library of Congress Cataloging-in-Publication Data

Careers in focus. Therapists. — 2nd ed.
   p. cm. — (Careers in focus)
 Includes bibliographical references and index.
 ISBN-13: 978-0-8160-7286-6 (alk. paper)
 ISBN-10: 0-8160-7286-8 (alk. paper)
 1. Allied health personnel—Vocational guidance. I. Ferguson Publishing. II. Title: Therapists.
 R697.A4C3735 2008
 610.69—dc22

                         2008003068

Ferguson books are available at special discounts when purchased in bulk quantities for businesses, associations, institutions, or sales promotions. Please call our Special Sales Department in New York at (212) 967-8800 or (800) 322-8755.

You can find Ferguson on the World Wide Web at http://www.fergpubco.com

Text design by David Strelecky
Cover design by Salvatore Luongo

Printed in the United States of America

MP MSRF 10 9 8 7 6 5 4 3 2 1

This book is printed on acid-free paper.

Table of Contents

Introduction

Therapists help injured, disabled, or emotionally disturbed people regain their strength to the fullest extent possible. There are many different kinds of therapists, each with special knowledge and special skills. *Art therapists*, for instance, use art to help resolve patients' physical, emotional, and social problems. *Grief therapists* counsel people who are mourning the death of a family member or loved one. *Physical therapists* help their patients to restore mobility, alleviate pain, and avoid permanent disability. *Rehabilitation counselors* help disabled people address life and work issues. *Respiratory therapists and technicians* assist patients who have deficiencies or abnormalities of the cardiopulmonary system. In short, there is a therapist for almost any type of physical or emotional disability. Therapists are valued health care professionals.

Educational requirements vary for therapists. Some therapist positions, such as *aromatherapists, hypnotherapists,* and *massage therapists,* require only some postsecondary training, while other positions, such as *occupational therapists* and *physical therapists,* require workers to have earned a bachelor's or master's degree, respectively.

Therapists work in a variety of settings, including private offices, hospitals, clinics, managed-care facilities, nursing homes, and private homes. According to the U.S. Department of Labor, employment in the health services industry is projected to increase by 27 percent through 2014—nearly double the growth predicted for all industries.

Most therapy careers have bright employment outlooks. Therapy careers that will enjoy especially strong growth include *aromatherapists, biofeedback therapists, grief therapists, massage therapists, myotherapists, occupational therapists, occupational therapy assistants and aides, orientation and mobility specialists, physical therapists, physical therapy assistants, rehabilitation counselors,* and *respiratory therapists and technicians.*

Each article in *Careers in Focus: Therapists* discusses a particular therapy occupation in detail. The articles appear in Ferguson's *Encyclopedia of Careers and Vocational Guidance* but have been updated and revised with the latest information from the U.S. Department of Labor and other sources.

The following paragraphs detail the sections and features that appear in the book.

The **Quick Facts** section provides a brief summary of the career, including recommended school subjects, personal skills, work environment, minimum educational requirements, salary ranges, certification or licensing requirements, and employment outlook. This section also provides acronyms and identification numbers for the following government classification indexes: the *Dictionary of Occupational Titles* (DOT), the *Guide for Occupational Exploration* (GOE), the National Occupational Classification (NOC) Index, and the Occupational Information Network (O*NET)-Standard Occupational Classification System (SOC) index. The DOT, GOE, and O*NET-SOC indexes have been created by the U.S. government; the NOC index is Canada's career classification system. Readers can use the identification numbers listed in the Quick Facts section to access further information about a career. Print editions of the DOT (*Dictionary of Occupational Titles*. Indianapolis, Ind.: JIST Works, 1991) and GOE (*Guide for Occupational Exploration*. Indianapolis, Ind.: JIST Works, 2001) are available at libraries. Electronic versions of the NOC (http://www23.hrdc-drhc.gc.ca) and O*NET-SOC (http://online.onetcenter.org) are available on the Internet. When no DOT, GOE, NOC, or O*NET-SOC numbers are present, this means that the U.S. Department of Labor or Human Resources Development Canada have not created a numerical designation for this career. In this instance, you will see the acronym "N/A," or not available.

The **Overview** section is a brief introductory description of the duties and responsibilities involved in this career. Oftentimes, a career may have a variety of job titles. When this is the case, alternative career titles are presented. Employment statistics are also provided, when available.

The **History** section describes the history of the particular job as it relates to the overall development of its industry or field.

The Job describes the primary and secondary duties of the job.

Requirements discusses high school and postsecondary education and training requirements, any certification or licensing that is necessary, and other personal requirements for success in the job.

Exploring offers suggestions on how to gain experience in or knowledge of the particular job before making a firm educational and financial commitment. The focus is on what can be done while still in high school (or in the early years of college) to gain a better understanding of the job.

The **Employers** section gives an overview of typical places of employment for the job.

Starting Out discusses the best ways to land that first job, be it through the college career services office, newspaper ads, Internet employment sites, or personal contact.

The **Advancement** section describes what kind of career path to expect from the job and how to get there. **Earnings** lists salary ranges and describes the typical fringe benefits.

The **Work Environment** section describes the typical surroundings and conditions of employment—whether indoors or outdoors, noisy or quiet, social or independent. Also discussed are typical hours worked, any seasonal fluctuations, and the stresses and strains of the job.

The **Outlook** section summarizes the job in terms of the general economy and industry projections. For the most part, Outlook information is obtained from the U.S. Bureau of Labor Statistics and is supplemented by information gathered from professional associations. Job growth terms follow those used in the *Occupational Outlook Handbook*. Growth described as "much faster than the average" means an increase of 27 percent or more. Growth described as "faster than the average" means an increase of 18 to 26 percent. Growth described as "about as fast as the average" means an increase of 9 to 17 percent. Growth described as "more slowly than the average" means an increase of 0 to 8 percent. "Decline" means a decrease by any amount. Each article ends with **For More Information,** which lists organizations that provide information on training, education, internships, scholarships, and job placement.

Careers in Focus: Therapists also includes photographs of professionals in various therapy professions, informative sidebars, and interviews with workers in the field.

Aromatherapists

OVERVIEW

Aromatherapists are health care specialists who use essential plant oils to promote health in their clients. Essential oils are highly concentrated substances that give plants their fragrance. These substances are extracted from various parts of aromatic plants, such as roots, woods, seeds, fruits, leaves, and flowers. Only about 5 percent of all types of plants are used for their essential oils.

Since the early 20th century, the professions of cosmetology, medicine, and psychology have rediscovered the healing powers of essential oils that were known to earlier civilizations. Scientific studies show that inhaling the fragrance of certain essential oils has physiological and psychological effects on the brain. Aromatherapists study the oils and their effects on individuals. They use this knowledge to help improve their clients' quality of life.

Most aromatherapists are licensed in other areas of health care or body care, using aromatherapy as a supplementary tool in their licensed profession. Among these licensed professionals are beauticians, chiropractors, cosmeticians, massage therapists, medical doctors, naturopathic doctors, nurse practitioners, and nurses. A few individuals who specialize in aromatherapy work as chemists, educators, or authors. A very few grow plants for the distillation of essential oils, become consultants, or start their own lines of aromatherapy products.

QUICK FACTS

School Subjects
Biology
Chemistry
English

Personal Skills
Helping/teaching
Technical/scientific

Work Environment
Primarily indoors
Primarily one location

Minimum Education Level
Some postsecondary training

Salary Range
$13,290 to $45,000 to
$80,000+

Certification or Licensing
Voluntary

Outlook
Faster than the average

DOT
N/A

GOE
N/A

NOC
3232

O*NET-SOC
N/A

HISTORY

Humanity's use of fragrance probably began long before recorded history. Anthropologists think that primitive people burned gums

5

and resin as incense. Throughout history, civilizations have used essential oils for many purposes—including healing. As an art and science, aromatherapy finds its roots in ancient cultures, dating back 4,000 to 5,000 years. Early Egyptians are often credited with being the first to make an art of the use of essential oils. They used myrrh and frankincense (fragrant resins from trees) in their daily rituals. However, other early cultures also used essential oils. In ancient Africa, people discovered that certain plants provided protection from the sun when they were rubbed on the skin. Chinese, Indian, Persian, and other African cultures used plant oils for incense burning, cooking, cosmetics, mummifying, bathing, perfumery, meditating, and healing.

In the spas of ancient Rome, oils were used in public baths and were applied during massages. The knowledge of oils went along with the spread of Roman culture. Europeans used oils during medieval times to fight disease. During the Middle Ages, the appearance of chemistry and the improvement of distillation helped simplify the process of extracting essential oils from plants. This opened the door to oil trading, which spread the new practices to more people and places.

Until the 19th century, when science began to introduce other medicines, Europeans used essential oils both as perfumes and for medicinal purposes. With the growth of newer medical practices, doctors began to choose modern medicine over the tradition of oils. It was not until the 20th century that several individuals "rediscovered" the healing power of essential oils. Once again the use of oils was integrated into Western culture.

In 1928, the French perfumer and chemist, René-Maurice Gattefossé, experienced the healing power of essential oils. When he severely burned his hand, he stuck it into the nearest liquid, which happened to be lavender oil. He was surprised how quickly the hand healed. His experience caused him to become interested in the therapeutic use of essential oils. It was Gattefossé who coined the term *aromatherapy*.

Dr. Jean Valnet, a French physician, was the first to reintegrate essential oils into Western medical practice. Dr. Valnet served as an army surgeon during World War II. Inspired by the work of Gattefossé, he used essential oils to treat the soldiers' burns and wounds. He also successfully treated psychiatric problems with fragrances.

Marguerite Maury, an Austrian biochemist, was also influenced by the work of Gattefossé. She integrated the use of essential oils into cosmetics.

In 1977, Robert Tisserand, an expert in aromatherapy, wrote *The Art of Aromatherapy*. Tisserand was strongly influenced by the work of both Gattefossé and Valnet. His book caught the interest of the American public and made a major contribution to the growth of aromatherapy in this country.

The Western world has rediscovered the uses of essential oils and fragrances through the work of people like Valnet, Maury, and Tisserand. In France, aromatherapy is practiced by medical doctors. Conventional and alternative medicine practitioners in England, Australia, Sweden, Japan, the United States, and other parts of the world are recognizing and utilizing the healing power of essential oils. The world is reawakening to the healing and life-enhancing capabilities of aromatherapy.

THE JOB

Whether aromatherapists work primarily as beauticians, chiropractors, massage therapists, or doctors, they must possess a strong working knowledge of aromatherapy as a science and an art. They need to understand the components and healing benefits of many essential oils. The quality of essential oils varies greatly depending on the plant, where it is grown, the conditions under which it is grown, and other factors. As a result, aromatherapists must be very careful about choosing the sources from which their oils come. Pure, high-quality, therapeutic grade oils are essential to good aromatherapy. Aromatherapists must even know the differences between the oils of different species of the same plant. Essential oils are very powerful because of their high concentration. It may take well over 100 pounds of plant material to produce just one pound of essential oil.

Because of the powerful concentration of essential oils, aromatherapists use great care in diluting them and in adding them to what are called carrier oils. These are most often high-quality vegetable oils, such as almond, olive, or sesame. Unlike essential oils, carrier oils are fixed, rather than volatile. A small amount of an essential oil is blended into the carrier oil, which "carries" it across the body. Aromatherapists are especially careful when the oils are to be applied to a client's skin or put into a bath. In addition, aromatherapists must know how different essential oils work together because they are often combined to achieve certain results.

Aromatherapists need to know much more than what oils to use. They use the essential oils in three types of aromatherapy: cosmetic, massage, and olfactory. Aromatherapists have to know the differences among the types of therapy. They must decide which type or combination of types to use in a particular situation, and they must be skilled in each type.

Aromatherapists must know how the body, mind, and emotions work together. For example, a client who complains of muscle tension may need physical relief. A massage with relaxing oils that the skin soaks in will relax the client. However, aromatherapists are able to take this treatment a step further. They consider the underlying causes of the condition. Why is the client feeling tense? Is it stress? Anxiety? Strong emotion? Massage therapists who are trained in aromatherapy may inquire about the client's life in order to pinpoint the source of the tension. Once the source is identified, aromatherapists utilize specific oils to produce a certain emotional effect in the client. When the scents of these oils are inhaled, they create a response within the entire body. The oils may be added to a bath or a compress that is applied to the body. A compress is a towel soaked in water that has a bit of an essential oil added to it. An aroma may take the client back to happier times, as a reminder of warmth, comfort, and contentment.

An aromatherapist's client may have skin problems due to stress. The aromatherapist may use certain essential oils to help both the skin condition on the surface and the underlying emotional source of the problem. This might be accomplished through olfactory aromatherapy—the inhalation of the oil vapors.

In a hospital, nursing home, or hospice setting, an aromatherapist might choose essential oils that help relieve stress. In England, hospital nursing staffs utilize essential oil massage. This type of therapy has been shown to relieve pain and induce sleep. Essential oil massage has proven effective in relieving the stress that patients experience with general illness, surgery, terminal cancer, and AIDS. Aromatherapists emphasize that these treatments are supplementary and enhancing to medical care—they do not replace medical treatment.

No two clients' problems are the same, and neither are the remedies for those problems. Each client must be treated as an individual. During the first visit, aromatherapists usually take a careful client history. Aromatherapists must listen carefully both for things their clients say and for things they don't say. Aromatherapists need to know if a client is taking any medicine or using any natural healing substances, such as herbs. They must understand the properties of the essential oils and how they might interact with any other treatment the client is using. Next, they use the information gathered from the client interview to determine the proper essential oils and the appropriate amounts to blend to serve the client's particular needs.

Aromatherapists are employed in a number of different work environments. Those connected to the beauty industry may work in salons, spas, or hotel resorts, incorporating aromatherapy into facial care, body care, and hair care. In the health care field, many professionals are turning to alternative approaches to care, and some conventional medical practitioners are beginning to implement more holistic approaches. As a result, a growing number of aromatherapists work in the offices of other health care specialists, where their aromatherapy treatments complement the other therapies used. Aromatherapists often give seminars, teach, or serve as consultants. Some who become experts on essential oils buy farms to grow plants for the oils, create their own lines of aromatherapy products, or sell essential oils to other aromatherapists.

REQUIREMENTS

High School

If you are interested in working with aromatherapy, begin in high school by building up your knowledge of the human body's systems. Biology, anatomy, and physiology will help lay the foundation for a career in aromatherapy. Chemistry courses will familiarize you with laboratory procedures. Aromatherapists need to have an understanding of mixtures and the care involved in using powerful essential oils. Chemistry can help you gain the experience you need to handle delicate or volatile substances. It will also familiarize you with the properties of natural compounds.

Keep in mind that the majority of aromatherapists are self-employed. Math, business, and computer courses will help you develop the skills you need to be successful at running a business. Aromatherapists also need good communication and interpersonal skills to be sensitive to their clients. English, speech, and psychology classes can help you sharpen your ability to interact constructively with other people.

Eva-Marie Lind is an aromatherapist, author, and former Dean of the Aromatherapy Department of the Australasian College of Herbal Studies in Lake Oswego, Oregon. She has worked in the field of aromatherapy for over 15 years. According to Lind, "Education is the key to good aromatherapy. There is so much to learn, and it takes real dedication to study."

Postsecondary Training

In 1999, the National Association for Holistic Aromatherapy (NAHA) established criteria for aromatherapy education that have been voluntarily adopted by a number of schools and education programs. NAHA guidelines recommend that aromatherapy education include courses on topics such as the history of aromatherapy, physiology, production of essential oils, botany, chemistry, safety and methods of application, and business planning.

While the NAHA provides a listing of schools complying with its guidelines, there are also other schools, seminars, and distance learning courses that offer training in aromatherapy. Be aware, however, that the quality of programs can vary. Take the time to call the schools or organizations that interest you. Ask how their programs are set up. For correspondence courses (or distance courses), ask if you will be able to talk to a teacher. How will you be evaluated? Are there tests? How are the tests taken and graded? Try to talk with current students. Ask how they are treated and what they learn. Ask what you receive when you graduate from the program. Will you receive help with job placement? Access to insurance programs? Other benefits? Depending on the program you pick, the length of study ranges from short workshops to four-year college courses. Vocational schools, major universities, and naturopathic colleges are increasingly offering training in aromatherapy.

Most aromatherapists are also professionals in other fields. Consider whether you would want to combine aromatherapy with a "base" profession, such as chiropractic, massage therapy, nursing, or some other field into which you might incorporate it. These base fields require additional education and certification as well as licensing. If you decide to add aromatherapy to another profession, learn the requirements for certification or licensing that apply to that profession. Adding aromatherapy to another profession requires a comprehensive understanding of both fields from a scientific standpoint.

Certification or Licensing

The Aromatherapy Registration Council offers voluntary registration to aromatherapists who meet minimum educational standards from an NAHA-approved academic institution and pass an examination, which focuses on four knowledge areas: Basic Concepts of Aromatherapy, Scientific Principles, Administration, and Professional Issues. Registration must be renewed every five years. Contact the council for more information on registration requirements.

If you choose to combine aromatherapy with another profession, you must meet the national and local requirements for that field in addition to aromatherapy requirements.

Other Requirements

According to Eva-Marie Lind, "Aromatherapy demands love and passion at its roots. You need to honor, respect, and celebrate the beauty of this field."

You must also enjoy disseminating knowledge because clients often have many questions. More practically, it takes a good nose and a certain sensitivity to successfully treat clients through aromatherapy. It takes good listening skills and immense creativity to understand each client's personal issues and decide on the best means of administering a treatment. Which essential oils or combination of oils should you choose? Should you use a bath, a compress, a massage, or inhalation? What parts of the body are the best avenues for delivering the remedy?

Aromatherapists must be good self-teachers who are interested in continuing education. This is a relatively new field that is developing and changing rapidly. To stay competitive and successful, you need to keep up with the changing trends, products, and technologies that affect the field. Like most healing professions, aromatherapy is a lifelong education process for the practitioner.

EXPLORING

There are many ways to explore the field of aromatherapy to see if it is for you. For one, there are many books and specialized periodicals available on the subject. These will help you to get a glimpse of the types of knowledge you need for the field. Find out whether it is too scientific or not scientific enough. Look in your local library for books and magazines that show you what a typical student of aromatherapy might be learning.

Visit health food stores. The staff members of health food stores are often very helpful. Most have books, magazines, and newspapers about many kinds of alternative health care, including aromatherapy. Ask about essential oils, and ask for the names of aromatherapists in the area. Find out if there are garden clubs that you can join—particularly ones that specialize in herbs. Consider taking up cooking. This could give you practice in selecting herbs and seasonings and blending them to create different aromas and flavors.

Contact local and national professional organizations. Some offer student memberships or free seminars. Check out their Web sites. They have a lot of valuable information and good links to other alternative health care sites. Join online forums and discussion groups where you can communicate with professionals from all over the country and the world. Some distance learning courses are open to students of all ages. Check into them.

If you find you have a real interest in aromatherapy, another way to explore the field is to seek a mentor, a professional in the field who is willing to help you learn. Tell everyone you know

The Top Essential Oils

Essential Oil	Health Benefits
Clary Sage	Reduces pain and achy muscles, helps with insomnia
Eucalyptus	Boosts respiratory and immune systems
Geranium	Hormone balance for women, antidepressant
Lavender	Treats burns and wounds, good for overall skin care
Lemon	Treats wounds and infections
Peppermint	Treats muscle pain, headaches, and some digestive disorders
Roman Chamomile	Reduces insomnia and anxiety, treats wounds and infections
Rosemary	Provides mental stimulation, boosts immune system, reduces muscle aches and tension
Tea Tree	Antifungal properties, boosts immune system
Ylang Ylang	Reduces muscle tension, helps fight depression

Source: National Association for Holistic Aromatherapy

that you are interested in aromatherapy. Someone is bound to have a connection with someone you could call for an informational interview. Perhaps you could spend a day "shadowing" an aromatherapist to see what the work is like. If you are unable to find an aromatherapy specialist, you could call spas and salons in search of professionals who use aromatherapy in their work. Perhaps some would be willing to speak to you about their day-to-day work. Make an appointment and experience an aromatherapy treatment. Taking it a step further, you could explore the possibility of getting a part-time job at an establishment that employs aromatherapists.

EMPLOYERS

Most aromatherapists are self-employed. They run their own small businesses and build their own clientele. Some set up their own offices, but many build their businesses by working in the offices of other professionals and giving aromatherapy treatments as supplements to the treatments provided by the resident professionals.

Many different kinds of employers are looking for skilled aromatherapists. In the cosmetic industry, beauticians, cosmeticians, and massage therapists employ aromatherapists to give treatments that complement their own. Spas, athletic clubs, resorts, and cruise ships may hire aromatherapists on a full-time basis. These types of employment may be temporary or seasonal.

In the health care industry, chiropractors, acupuncturists, and other alternative therapy practitioners and clinics may offer aromatherapy in addition to their basic services. Hospitals, nursing homes, hospice centers, and other medical establishments are beginning to recognize the physiological and psychological benefits of aromatherapy for their patients.

STARTING OUT

Because the practice of aromatherapy may be incorporated into numerous other professions, there are many ways to enter the field. How you enter depends on how you want to use aromatherapy. Is your interest in massage therapy, skin care, or hair care? Do you want to be a nurse, doctor, acupuncturist, or chiropractor? Are you interested in becoming an instructor or writer? Once you are certified in another area, you need to search for clinics, salons, spas, and other establishments that are looking for professionals who use aromatherapy in their treatments. School career services offices are also ways to find work. Classified ads in newspapers and trade magazines list positions in the related fields.

Networking can be an important source of job opportunities. Networking is simply getting to know others and exchanging ideas with them. Go to association meetings and conventions. Talk to people in the field. Job openings are often posted at such gatherings.

ADVANCEMENT

Aromatherapists can advance to many different levels, depending on their goals, ambitions, aspirations, and willingness to work. Those who are self-employed can increase their clientele and open their own offices or even a salon. Those who are employed at a spa or salon could become a department director or the director of the entire spa or salon. They might start a private practice or open a spa or salon.

As their skills and knowledge grow, aromatherapists may be sought after to teach and train other aromatherapists in seminars or at schools that offer aromatherapy programs or courses. Others become consultants or write books and articles. A few start their own aromatherapy product lines of esthetic or therapeutic products. Some may become involved in growing the plants that are the sources of essential oils. Still others work in distilling, analyzing, or blending the oils.

This new field is growing so rapidly that the potential for advancement is enormous. The field has so many facets that the directions for growth are as great as your imagination and determination. A public relations representative from the National Association for Holistic Aromatherapy says, "If you are self-motivated, creative, and have a talent for any aspect of aromatherapy, the sky is the limit. It is what you make it."

EARNINGS

Since aromatherapists work in such a variety of settings, and aromatherapy is often a supplementary therapy added to other professional training, it is particularly difficult to make statements about average earnings in the field. Government agencies do not yet have wage statistics for the field. The national professional associations have not yet developed surveys of their members that give reliable information.

For those who are self-employed in any profession, earnings depend on the amount of time they work and the amount they charge per hour. Experienced professional aromatherapists estimate that hourly rates can range from $25 to $65 for beginning aromatherapists and instructors. Rates increase with experience to between $75 and $100 per hour. Based on those rates, a beginning aromatherapist who charges $25 an hour and averages 10 appointments per week will earn around $13,000. According to the U.S. Department of Labor, in 2006 the median annual salary for people engaged in personal care and service occupations (the category aromatherapy would fall into) earned a median salary of $19,070, with the bottom 10 percent earning $13,290 or less per year and the top 10 percent $36,940 or more. Established aromatherapists who have a solid client base report earning $25,000 to $45,000.

The hourly rate an aromatherapist charges depends on his or her level of expertise, the type of clientele served, and even the area of the country. In many of the larger cities and much of the West Coast, people are already more aware and accepting of alternative health therapies. In those areas, higher hourly rates will be more accepted. Where such therapies are practically unknown, lower rates will apply. Another consideration for the self-employed is that they must provide their own insurance and retirement plans and pay for their supplies and other business expenses.

An aromatherapist with determination, creativity, and initiative can find jobs that pay well. Some who run exclusive spas or develop their own lines of aromatherapy products are reported to earn $70,000 to $80,000 or more.

Aromatherapists who are primarily employed in other professions, such as massage therapists, chiropractors, cosmetologists, and nurses, can expect to make the salaries that are average for their profession. Those professionals who use aromatherapy as a supportive therapy to their primary profession tend to have higher incomes than those who specialize in aromatherapy. The addition of aromatherapy to their profession will probably enhance their clients' and their own satisfaction, but it may not increase their income.

WORK ENVIRONMENT

Aromatherapists work in a service-oriented environment, in which their main duty involves understanding and helping their clients. The surroundings are usually clean, peaceful, and pleasant. They work with very potent substances (strong essential oils), but most aromatherapists love the scents and the experience of the oils. They often spend a great deal of time on their feet. They sometimes work long or inconsistent hours, such as weekends and evenings, to accommodate their clients' needs.

Aromatherapists are people-oriented. Those who are self-employed must be highly motivated and able to work alone. Aromatherapists who work in clinics, spas, hospitals, resorts, and other locations need to be able to work well with others.

OUTLOOK

Aromatherapy has been growing very rapidly and is gathering steam in the United States. Opportunities are increasing rapidly as public awareness of alternative therapies is increasing.

The status of aromatherapy in European and other countries may provide a glimpse of the future of the field in the United States. In Great Britain and France, for example, more doctors have embraced aromatherapy, and these services are covered by major health plans. If the United States follows this lead, new doors will open in this field. In general, the outlook is very good for aromatherapy because of an overwhelming increase in public awareness and interest.

FOR MORE INFORMATION

For information regarding state regulations for massage therapists and general information on therapeutic massage, contact
American Massage Therapy Association
500 Davis Street, Suite 900
Evanston, IL 60201-4695
Tel: 877-905-2700
Email: info@amtamassage.org
http://www.amtamassage.org

For information on registration, contact
Aromatherapy Registration Council
5940 SW Hood Avenue
Portland, OR 97039-3719
Tel: 503-244-0726
Email: info@aromatherapycouncil.org
http://www.aromatherapycouncil.org

The National Association for Holistic Aromatherapy has developed guidelines for aromatherapy training. See its Web site for a listing of schools in compliance with these guidelines.
National Association for Holistic Aromatherapy
3327 West Indian Trail Road, PMB 144
Spokane, WA 99208-4762
Tel: 509-325-3419
Email: info@naha.org
http://www.naha.org

For general information about aromatherapy and education options, visit the following Web site:
AromaWeb
http://www.aromaweb.com

Art Therapists

OVERVIEW

Art therapists treat and rehabilitate people with mental, physical, and emotional disabilities. They use the creative processes of art in their therapy sessions to determine the underlying causes of problems and to help patients achieve therapeutic goals. Therapists usually specialize in one particular type of therapeutic activity, such as painting, sculpture, or photography. The specific objectives of the therapeutic activities vary according to the needs of the patient and the setting of the therapy program.

HISTORY

Creative arts therapy programs are fairly recent additions to the health care field. Although many theories of mental and physical therapy have existed for centuries, it has been only in the last 70 years or so that health care professionals have truly realized the healing powers of art, as well as music, dance, and other forms of artistic self-expression.

Art therapy is based on the idea that people who can't discuss their problems with words must have another outlet for self-expression. In the early 1900s, psychiatrists began to look more closely at their patients' artwork, realizing that there could be links between the emotional or psychological illness and the art. Sigmund Freud even did some preliminary research into the artistic expression of his patients.

In the 1930s, art educators discovered that children often expressed their thoughts better with pictures and role-playing than they did through verbalization. Children often don't know the words they

QUICK FACTS

School Subjects
Art
Sociology
Technical/shop

Personal Skills
Artistic
Helping/teaching

Work Environment
Primarily indoors
Primarily one location

Minimum Education Level
Master's degree

Salary Range
$20,880 to $45,000 to $100,000

Certification or Licensing
Recommended (certification)
Required by all states (licensing)

Outlook
About as fast as the average

DOT
076

GOE
14.06.01

NOC
3144

O*NET-SOC
29-1125.00

need to explain how they feel or how to make their needs known to adults. Researchers began to look into art as a way to treat children who were traumatized by abuse, neglect, illness, or other physical or emotional disabilities.

During and after World War II, the Department of Veterans Affairs (VA) developed and organized various arts activities for patients in VA hospitals. These activities had a dramatic effect on the physical and mental well-being of the World War II veterans, and art therapists began to help treat and rehabilitate patients in other health care settings.

Because of early breakthroughs with children and veterans, the number of art therapists has increased greatly over the past few decades, and the field has expanded to include drama, psychodrama, and poetry, in addition to the original areas of music, art, and dance. Today, art therapists work with diverse populations of patients in a wide range of facilities, and they focus on the specific needs of a vast spectrum of disorders and disabilities. Colleges and universities offer degree programs in many types of therapies, and national associations for registering and certifying creative arts therapists work to monitor training programs and to ensure the professional integrity of the therapists.

THE JOB

Similar to dreaming, art therapy taps into the subconscious and gives people a mode of expression in an uncensored environment. This is important because before patients can begin to heal, they must first identify their feelings. Once they recognize their feelings, they can begin to develop an understanding of the relationship between their feelings and their behavior.

The main goal of an art therapist is to improve the client's physical, mental, and emotional health. Before therapists begin any treatment, they meet with a team of other health care professionals. After determining the strength, limitations, and interests of their client, they create a program to promote positive change and growth. The therapist continues to confer with the other health care workers as the program progresses, and alters the program according to the client's progress. How these goals are reached depends on the unique specialty of the therapist in question.

"It's like sitting in the woods waiting for a fawn to come out." That is how Barbara Fish, former director of activity therapy for the Illinois Department of Mental Health and Developmental Disabilities, Chicago Metropolitan and Adolescent Services, describes her experience as she waits patiently for a sexually abused patient to begin to trust her. The patient is extraordinarily frightened because of the traumatic abuse she has suffered. This may be the first time in the patient's life that she is in an environment of acceptance and support. It may take months or even years before the patient begins to trust the therapist, "come out of the woods," and begin to heal.

In some cases, especially when the clients are adolescents, they may have become so detached from their feelings that they can physically act out without consciously knowing the reasons for their behavior. This detachment from their emotions creates a great deal of psychological pain. With the help of an art therapist, clients can begin to communicate their subconscious feelings both verbally and nonverbally. They can express their emotions in a variety of ways, through painting, sketching, sculpting, or other art forms, without having to name them.

Art therapists work with all age groups: young children, adolescents, adults, and senior citizens. They can work in individual, group, or family sessions. The approach of the therapist, however, depends on the specific needs of the client or group. For example, if an individual is feeling overwhelmed by too many options or stimuli, the therapist may give him or her only a plain piece of paper and a pencil to work with that day.

Fish has three ground rules for her art therapy sessions with disturbed adolescents: respect yourself, respect other people, and respect property. The therapy groups are limited to five patients per group. She begins the session by asking each person in the group how he or she is feeling that day. By carefully listening to their responses, a theme may emerge that will determine the direction of the therapy. For example, if anger is reoccurring in their statements, Fish may ask them to draw a line down the center of a piece of paper. On one side, she will ask them to draw how anger looks and on the other side how feeling sad looks. Then, once the drawing is complete, she will ask them to compare the two pictures and see that their anger may be masking their feelings of sadness, loneliness, and disappointment. As patients begin to recognize their true feelings, they develop better control of their behavior.

To reach their patients, art therapists use art lessons and projects to improve a patient's self-confidence and self-awareness, to relieve states of depression, and to improve physical dexterity. The art therapist encourages and teaches patients to express their thoughts, feelings, and anxieties via sketching, drawing, painting, or sculpting. Art therapy is especially helpful in revealing patterns of domestic abuse in families. Children involved in such a situation may depict

An art therapist works on an art project with a teenage girl in a residential respite care home. *(John Birdsall, The Image Works)*

scenes of family life with violent details or portray a certain family member as especially frightening or threatening.

Art can also be used with the elderly. An art therapist treating a patient with Alzheimer's might ask the client to draw a childhood home from his or her past, thus stimulating long- and short-term memory, soothing feelings of agitation, and increasing a sense of reality.

REQUIREMENTS

High School

To become an art therapist, you will need a bachelor's degree, so take a college preparatory curriculum while in high school. You should become as proficient as possible with the methods and tools related to the type of art therapy you wish to pursue. When therapists work with patients, they must be able to concentrate completely on the patient rather than on learning how to use tools or techniques. For example, if you want to become involved in therapy through sculpture, you need to be familiar with all the details of the craft before applying it to help patients.

In addition to art courses, you should consider taking an introductory class in psychology. Also, a communication class will give you an understanding of the various ways people communicate, both verbally and nonverbally.

Postsecondary Training

To become an art therapist, you must earn at least a bachelor's degree in studio art, art education, or psychology with a strong emphasis on art courses as well. In most cases, however, you will also need a graduate degree before you can gain certification as a professional or advance in your chosen field. Requirements for admission to graduate schools vary by program, so you would be wise to contact the graduate programs you are interested in to find out about their admissions policies. For some fields, you may be required to submit a portfolio of your work along with the written application. Professional organizations can be a good source of information regarding high-quality programs. For example, the American Art Therapy Association provides lists of schools that meet its standards for approval. (Contact information is listed at the end of this article.)

In graduate school, your study of psychology and art will be in-depth. Classes for a master's degree in art therapy may include group psychotherapy, foundation of creativity theory, assessment and treatment planning, and art therapy presentation. In addition to classroom study, you will also complete an internship or supervised practicum (that is, work with clients). Depending on your program, you may also need to write a thesis or present a final artistic project before receiving your degree.

Certification or Licensing

The Art Therapy Credentials Board offers registration and certification to art therapists. Therapists may receive the designation art therapist registered (ATR) after completing a graduate program and having some experience working with clients. For further certification, therapists can earn the designation art therapist registered–board certified (ATR-BC) by passing an additional written exam. To retain certification status, therapists must complete a certain amount of continuing education.

Many registered art therapists also hold additional licenses in other fields, such as social work, education, mental health, or marriage and family therapy. In some states, art therapists need licensing depending on their place of work. For specific information on licensing in your field, you will need to check with your state's licensing board. Therapists are also often members of other professional associations, including the American Psychological Association, the American Association for Marriage and Family Therapy, and the American Counseling Association.

Other Requirements

To succeed in this line of work, you should have a strong desire to help others seek positive change in their lives. All art therapists must be able to work well with other people—both patients and other health professionals—in the development and implementation of therapy programs. You must have the patience and the stamina to teach and practice therapy with patients for whom progress is often very slow because of their various physical and emotional disorders. A therapist must always keep in mind that even a tiny amount of progress might be extremely significant for some patients and their families. A good sense of humor is also a valuable trait.

EXPLORING

There are many ways to explore the possibility of a career as an art therapist. You could write to professional associations for information on therapy careers. Talk with people working in the field and perhaps arrange to observe a therapy session. Look for part-time or summer jobs or volunteer at a hospital, clinic, nursing home, or any of a number of health care facilities.

A summer job as an aide at a camp for disabled children, for example, can help provide insight into the nature of art therapy, including both its rewards and demands. Such experience can be very valuable in deciding if you are suited to the inherent frustrations of a therapy career.

EMPLOYERS

Art therapists usually work as members of an interdisciplinary health care team that may include physicians, nurses, social workers, psychiatrists, and psychologists. Although often employed in hospitals, therapists also work in rehabilitation centers, nursing homes, day treatment facilities, shelters for battered women, pain and stress management clinics, substance abuse programs, hospices, and correctional facilities. Others maintain their own private practices. Many art therapists work with children in grammar and high schools, either as general therapists or art teachers. Some art therapists teach or conduct research in the creative arts at colleges and universities.

STARTING OUT

After earning a bachelor's degree in art, psychology, or a related field, you should complete your certification, which may include an internship or assistantship. Unpaid training internships often can lead to a first job in the field. Graduates can use the career services office at their college or university to help them find positions in the art therapy field. Many professional associations also compile lists of job openings to assist their members.

Therapists who are new to the field might consider doing volunteer work at a nonprofit community organization, correctional facility, or neighborhood association to gain some practical experience. Therapists who want to start their own practice can host group therapy sessions in their homes. Art therapists may also wish to associate with other members of the alternative health care field in order to gain experience and build a client base.

ADVANCEMENT

With more experience, therapists can move into supervisory, administrative, and teaching positions. Often, the supervision of interns can resemble a therapy session. The interns will discuss their feelings and ask questions they may have regarding their work with clients. How did they handle their clients? What were the reactions to what their clients said or did? What could they be doing to help more? The supervising therapist helps the interns become competent art therapists.

Many therapists have represented the profession internationally. Barbara Fish was invited to present her paper, "Art Therapy with Children and Adolescents," at the University of Helsinki. Additionally, Fish spoke in Finland at a three-day workshop exploring the use and effectiveness of art therapy with children and adolescents. Raising the public and professional awareness of creative arts therapy is an important concern for many therapists.

EARNINGS

A therapist's annual salary depends on experience, level of training, and education. Working on a hospital staff or being self-employed also affects annual income.

According to the American Art Therapy Association (AATA), entry-level art therapists earn annual salaries of approximately $32,000. Median annual salaries are about $45,000, and AATA reports that top earnings for salaried administrators ranged from $50,000 and $100,000 annually. Those who have Ph.D.s and are licensed for private practice can earn between $75 and $150 per hour, according to AATA. However those in private practice must pay professional expenses such as insurance and office rental. The median annual earnings for recreational therapists, a category that includes art therapists, in 2006 were $34,990, according to the U.S. Department of Labor. The lowest paid 10 percent earned $20,880 or less, while the highest paid 10 percent earned $55,530 or more.

Benefits depend on the employer but generally include paid vacation time, health insurance, and paid sick days. Those who are in private practice must provide their own benefits.

WORK ENVIRONMENT

Most art therapists work a typical 40-hour, five-day workweek; at times, however, they may have to work extra hours. The number of patients under a therapist's care depends on the specific employment setting. Although many therapists work in hospitals, they may also be employed in such facilities as clinics, rehabilitation centers, children's homes, schools, and nursing homes. Some therapists maintain service contracts with several facilities. For instance, a therapist might work two days a week at a hospital, one day at a nursing home, and the rest of the week at a rehabilitation center.

Most buildings are pleasant, comfortable, and clean places in which to work. Experienced art therapists might choose to be self-employed, working with patients in their own studios. In such a case, the therapist might work more irregular hours to accommodate patient schedules. Other therapists might maintain a combination of service contract work with one or more facilities in addition to a private caseload of clients referred to them by other health care professionals. Whether therapists work on service contracts with various facilities or maintain private practices, they must deal with all of the business and administrative details and worries that go along with being self-employed.

OUTLOOK

The American Art Therapy Association notes that this is a growing field. Demand for new therapists is created as medical professionals and the general public become aware of the benefits gained through art therapies. Although enrollment in college therapy programs is increasing, new graduates are usually able to find jobs. In cases where an individual is unable to find a full-time position, a therapist might obtain service contracts for part-time work at several facilities.

Job openings in facilities such as nursing homes should continue to increase as the elderly population grows over the next few decades. Advances in medical technology and the recent practice of early discharge from hospitals should also create new opportunities in managed care facilities, chronic pain clinics, and cancer care facilities. The demand for therapists of all types should continue to increase as more people become aware of the need to help disabled patients in creative ways.

FOR MORE INFORMATION

For more information about art therapy, contact
   American Art Therapy Association
   5999 Stevenson Avenue
   Alexandria, VA 22304-3304
   Tel: 888-290-0878
   Email: info@arttherapy.org
   http://www.arttherapy.org

For more information on careers in psychology and to order books such as Career Paths in Psychology: Where Your Degree Can Take You, *contact*
   American Psychological Association
   750 First Street, NE
   Washington, DC 20002-4242
   Tel: 800-374-2721
   http://www.apa.org

For an overview of all forms of creative arts therapy, visit the NCCATA Web site:
   National Coalition of Creative Arts Therapies Associations (NCCATA)
   c/o AMTA
   8455 Colesville Road, Suite 1000
   Silver Spring, MD 20910-3392
   http://www.nccata.org

INTERVIEW

Dr. Marcia Rosal is chair of the Art Education Department and director of the Art Therapy Program at Florida State University in Tallahassee, Florida. She discussed art therapy with the editors of Careers in Focus: Therapists.

Q. Please tell us about your program and your background.

A. The Florida State University Art Therapy Program offers a master of science in art therapy as well as a concentration in art therapy on the doctoral level. The two-year program leads to registration and certification on the national level and eligibility for licensure on the state level. The philosophical focus of the program is a constructivist approach to learning, which allows students to gather information on a variety of approaches to art therapy and then develop their own approach. Students are in internship for a minimum of 800 hours during the program. This ensures that they are ready for employment at the end of the program. Students can elect to complete a thesis or a culminating project as the capstone of the program.

As the program director, my background is in art education and in educational psychology, as well as art therapy. I taught art to special needs students prior to studying art therapy.

Q. What made you want to become an art therapist?

A. As an art educator in a special needs classroom, it became clear that art was a successful tool for therapy and remediation as well as for education. I wanted to learn more about this process and decided to pursue an art therapy graduate degree.

Q. What is one thing that young people may not know about a career in art therapy?

A. Art therapists are creative individuals who pursue additional creative avenues in addition to working with special needs populations. Many pursue wellness and other health-related activities and use art therapy tools to maintain balance and wellness in their own lives.

Q. What are the most important qualities for art therapy majors?

A. Important personal qualities of art therapists include a natural sense of caring for those in need and having an inquiring mind. Of course, an artistic sensibility is also required. Students should also possess self-knowledge and be open to feedback.

Q. What advice would you give art therapy majors as they graduate and look for jobs?

A. Even though the profession of art therapy has been around for more than 40 years, new art therapists must be open to taking risks in a job search and must be ready to talk about their therapy skills in a broader context than just art therapy. As a graduate, they have the same therapy skills as other master's level clinicians. They should be able to discuss and demonstrate these skills and then add that they can work with those individuals who are not able to verbally participate in the therapeutic process. This skill makes art therapists very valuable to any treatment team.

Q. What is the employment outlook for art therapists?

A. There are numerous opportunities for art therapists if they follow the advice from above. Current changes in the job market mandate that art therapists be credentialed and eligible for licensure in the state in which they wish to practice. Working toward national credentials through the Art Therapy Credentials Board is a must. Students should discuss licensure issues with faculty and ensure that they have all the courses needed to be eligible for licensure in their state.

Biofeedback Therapists

OVERVIEW

Biofeedback training is a process that helps patients gain control of their responses to stress, anxiety, physical strain, and emotional stimuli. Special instruments monitor a variety of physiological conditions, including heart rate, skin temperature, muscle tension, and blood pressure. *Biofeedback therapists* assist patients in interpreting the information gathered through monitoring. They help them learn to control individual body functions and reactions in ways that can decrease stress and alleviate the effects of a wide range of disorders, such as migraine headaches, gastrointestinal concerns, and epilepsy.

HISTORY

Biofeedback therapy has a relatively short history. The term itself did not come into widespread use until roughly 1969, when the results of four separate lines of research converged into a new approach to the treatment of a variety of medical and psychological conditions.

Until the early 1960s, psychologists generally accepted the premise that biological responses typically thought to be "involuntary," or under the control of the autonomic nervous system (such as heart rate, stomach acid secretion, blood pressure, or skin resistance) could not be modified or influenced using measurable instrumental means. Instead, this form of conditioned learning was thought possible only for responses that were under "voluntary" control, such as skeletal muscle responses. A definitive statement of this collective assumption appeared in a 1961 textbook, prompting a number of scientists to begin studies to refute it.

QUICK FACTS

School Subjects
Biology
Psychology

Personal Skills
Helping/teaching
Technical/scientific

Work Environment
Primarily indoors
Primarily one location

Minimum Education Level
Bachelor's degree

Salary Range
$30,000 to $50,000 to $200,000

Certification or Licensing
Recommended

Outlook
Faster than the average

DOT
N/A

GOE
N/A

NOC
N/A

O*NET-SOC
N/A

Four areas of study in particular yielded notable results. One approach employed a shock-avoidance paradigm in which subjects could avoid mild electrical shocks by making appropriate adjustments in heart rate. These studies demonstrated that statistically significant increases and decreases in heart rate could be obtained using instrument-based conditioning techniques. Other work achieved similar results using a positive reinforcement paradigm rather than shock avoidance.

About the same time, several other researchers showed that *galvanic skin response*, the ability of the body to conduct minute amounts of naturally occurring electrical current across the skin, could also be controlled by individuals.

As these reports surfaced, critics began to appear. They pointed to the fact that some voluntary responses can elicit a response that appears to be autonomic or involuntary. For instance, changes in heart rate can be initiated by altering respiration patterns or tensing certain muscle groups—both responses under voluntary control. If changes in heart rate, an autonomically mediated response, were "caused" by changes in responses under voluntary control, critics argued, such a demonstration would not prove that heart rate itself could be changed by voluntary control.

A third line of research sought to address this concern, removing the effect of voluntary responses from the equation. Laboratory rats were injected with curare, a drug that paralyzes all skeletal muscles (including those that enable the animals to breathe). They then were maintained on artificial respiration, which kept them alive and exactly regulated their breathing. Finally, an electrode was implanted in the hypothalamus, the part of the brain that regulates body temperature, certain metabolic processes, and other involuntary activities, so the researchers could control its actions. With this preparation, scientists showed that several involuntary responses could be spontaneously conditioned—not only heart rate, but also blood pressure and urine formation, among others. This demonstration of large magnitude changes in the responses of the internal organs in animals encouraged researchers to speculate on the wide range of human psychosomatic disorders that might be treatable with biofeedback.

Eventually, a fourth avenue of research emerged in the field of electroencephalography (EEG), the study of electrical activity in the brain. Several scientists began to study whether subjects could "voluntarily" produce certain EEG patterns—particularly the *alpha rhythm*, a distinctive rhythm associated with deep relaxation. Because of the similarity in the subjective experience of a "high alpha state" with that reported for meditation, self-control of EEG patterns attracted much attention beyond the scientific community, helping the entire field to grow.

THE JOB

Biofeedback therapy is a treatment that over the last three decades has shown considerable promise for patients with a wide range of conditions and disorders. Because it can be adapted to so many uses, it has developed more as a complementary skill than as a separate career. Biofeedback therapists come from a variety of backgrounds— physicians, social workers, psychologists, physical therapists, chiropractors, speech pathologists, even dental hygienists, among others. These professionals incorporate biofeedback learning techniques into the more traditional treatments they regularly provide. While it is not impossible to have a career in biofeedback without underlying training in a different field, few people are trained only as biofeedback therapists. It is true, however, that many therapists with experience in other disciplines choose to focus their practices largely on biofeedback.

An understanding of the uses of biofeedback begins with an understanding of the effects of stress. Stress often arises from major life changes, such as divorce, the death of a loved one, a move to a new home, or even celebrating holidays with family. In such high-stress times, a person's body undergoes "fight-or-flight" reactions. The body reacts physiologically to a person's mental and emotional concerns.

The effects of a typical fight-or-flight situation, such as a mugging or assault, may be considerable. A person reacting to such a potentially life-threatening situation will experience physiological changes. But much smaller stresses to a person's system, such as anxiety the night before an important exam, can also have lingering negative effects. An exam is not a life-threatening situation, but if someone perceives it that way, these perceptions can cause the same types of physiological changes.

Some people are terrified to speak in front of a group. There is no physical danger, but the speaker feels threatened in nonphysical ways—he or she may trip, forget lines, mispronounce words, fail at getting a message across, or be ridiculed. The speaker becomes nervous and tense, activating the fight-or-flight response when there is no real reason to do so.

Scientists believe that if people can learn to make themselves ill in this way, by moving their body systems out of balance, they might very well be able to learn to reverse the process and make themselves well. Biofeedback training teaches patients to restore balance to their body systems by voluntarily controlling generally involuntary reactions to various forms of stress.

There are three primary forms of biofeedback therapy; they involve the measurement of skin temperature, muscle tension, and brain waves. Each form is useful in a different range of disorders and conditions, and the list continues to grow.

Skin temperature biofeedback is often used with a therapeutic technique called autogenic training. Skin temperature is affected by blood flow, which is affected by stress. When a person is tense, blood vessels narrow, limiting the flow of blood in the body and causing skin temperature to drop. Biofeedback therapists place sensors on the hands or feet to determine blood flow. *Autogenic training* involves mastering passive concentration, and when properly practiced, helps the patient relax deeply through a number of repeated formula phrases ("My right arm is heavy. My right arm is heavy. My right arm is heavy. My left arm is heavy..."). The relaxation improves blood flow and raises skin temperature. These techniques have been shown to aid patients suffering from severe migraine headaches, Raynaud's disease (a disorder of the blood vessels in the extremities characterized by extreme sensitivity to cold), and hypertension or high blood pressure, among other complaints.

Muscle tension biofeedback, or *electromyograph (EMG) biofeedback training,* involves using sensitive electrodes to detect the amount of electrical activity in muscles. Auditory and visual feedback helps patients learn to control the pace and intensity of this activity. Autogenic training may be used in these situations as well to encourage relaxation. Many disorders respond to EMG biofeedback therapy, including tension headaches, anxieties, phobias, and psychoses.

The last line of research is the study of brain waves using *electroencephalograph (EEG),* or *neurobiofeedback.* Brain waves display certain characteristic rhythmic patterns. *Beta rhythms* are fast and have small amplitude; they predominate when you are awake or mentally aroused. *Alpha rhythms,* the first to be identified in EEG biofeedback therapy, are extraordinarily symmetrical, have large amplitude, and increase in most patients when they close their eyes and relax their bodies. *Theta rhythms* continue the slide toward sleep and increase as a person becomes drowsy, corresponding to early dreaming states. *Delta rhythms* are irregular and occur in heavy, dreamless sleep. Biofeedback training that teaches patients to seek the alpha state has been shown to be helpful in the treatment of

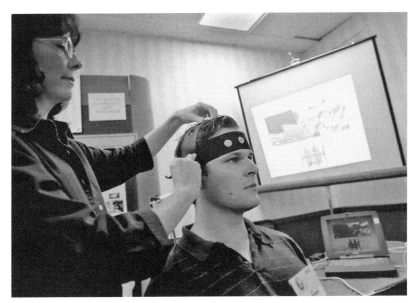

A biofeedback therapist places biofeedback sensors on a patient. *(Tony Savino, The Image Works)*

epilepsy, attention deficit disorder, autism, and obsessive-compulsive disorders, among other maladies. Scientists currently are exploring the use of EEG training in enhancing creativity and improving learning.

A biofeedback therapist's approach depends on his or her primary training. Physicians use biofeedback to complement medical remedies. Social workers use biofeedback to help patients cope with the social and emotional effects of chronic and sometimes debilitating problems. Music therapists use music and rhythm in conjunction with biofeedback to help patients understand and control physiological and emotional reactions. Other professionals who might use biofeedback therapy include nurses, psychiatrists, physical therapists, and anyone involved in health care or counseling work.

REQUIREMENTS
High School
To enter this range of careers you will need to take science courses, such as biology and anatomy. Physical education and health will give you some understanding of the physical aspects of biofeedback. Since counseling skills are also important, classes in psychology and sociology can be helpful.

Biofeedback currently is a rapidly expanding field. The marriages of art and biofeedback (as in an art therapy practice) or sports and biofeedback (as in the development of specialized training programs for top athletes) are just two of the many more unusual applications of this discipline.

Postsecondary Training

Most people who practice biofeedback therapy first become licensed in some other area of health care. Biofeedback then becomes an area of specialization within their practices. A biofeedback therapist may have a master's degree in social work, a Ph.D. in psychology, a nursing or medical degree, or some other professional designation. After receiving this professional degree (which may take 10 or more years, in the case of a medical degree), you then take courses in biofeedback from approved schools.

The Biofeedback Certification Institute of America (BCIA) provides a listing of approved schools and required course work on its Web site (http://www.bcia.org). Though many institutions offer workshops in biofeedback and may even offer biofeedback training programs and degrees, not all of them are approved by the certifying board. Some biofeedback therapists do practice without certification, but these uncertified therapists are not recognized by the professional organizations.

Certification or Licensing

The BCIA was created to establish and maintain standards for practitioners who use biofeedback and to certify practitioners who meet those standards. BCIA certification requires you to have a minimum of a bachelor's degree granted by a regionally accredited academic institution in one of the following approved health care fields: counseling, chiropractic, dental hygiene, dentistry, exercise physiology, medicine, nursing (note: licensed RNs are accepted with an associate's degree), occupational therapy, physical therapy, physician's assistant, psychology, recreational therapy, rehabilitation, respiratory therapy, social work, speech pathology, and sports medicine. Those who do not have a degree in one of these fields may be eligible for certification through a special review.

Candidates must complete training at an accredited biofeedback training program. This involves coursework as well as hands-on experience. Class work covers topics such as neuromuscular intervention, the autonomic nervous system, and professional conduct. The clinical training involves working directly with patients while under careful supervision and using a variety of biofeedback techniques. Candidates must also receive biofeedback, have supervised patient case conferences, and complete a comprehensive course in human anatomy, human biology, or human physiology. Once all of these requirements are fulfilled, candidates are eligible to take the rigorous written certification exam.

At this time, BCIA certification is not mandatory, but is recommended. In addition to its general program, the BCIA offers specialty certifications in EEG biofeedback and pelvic muscle dysfunction biofeedback.

Other Requirements

The practice of biofeedback therapy involves a great deal of personal interaction. As a result, you must enjoy being around a variety of people. Biofeedback practitioners also need excellent communication skills and must be careful listeners, able to pay attention to details. A genuine empathy for patients is important as well. Because biofeedback is a growing but still fairly new field, business and management skills will be important. Therapists generally are responsible for building their own practices, and like most other health care professionals, typically spend many hours dealing with insurance, managed care, and financial issues.

EXPLORING

You can begin exploring this field by contacting and interviewing biofeedback therapists in your area to gain a more specific understanding of their day-to-day activities.

If your school participates in an annual science fair, consider using the opportunity to develop a presentation on biofeedback. Many simple experiments are possible and appropriate for this setting. (Consider a sophisticated take on mood rings, for instance.)

Outside school, you can practice a number of forms of noninstrumental biofeedback. Yoga and Zen meditation both will help you become more attuned to your own body and its rhythms—an important skill to have as a biofeedback therapist. Learning either of these disciplines will give you a taste of how body systems can be trained to respond to intention and outside control and will teach you how to recognize some of your own body's feedback patterns.

EMPLOYERS

Biofeedback therapy has been shown to be useful in the treatment of such a wide variety of conditions and disorders that therapists can be found in a number of background specialties, from medicine and psychology to occupational therapy and dentistry. This means that biofeedback therapists are employed by many different types of institutions. They often have private practices as well. If you can envision ways in which biofeedback can assist people in whatever career field you might find yourself, chances are you can build a practice around it, either alone, or working with a group or for an institutional employer. Medical centers are the most common place of employment for biofeedback therapists, but more and more corporations are finding applications for biofeedback in the workplace.

STARTING OUT

Most biofeedback therapists come to the discipline with established practices in other fields. Once you have received the minimum of a bachelor's degree in your primary field, you can begin to think about specific training in biofeedback therapy. (A master's or sometimes even a doctorate is preferred to a bachelor's, depending on your areas of study.)

BCIA certification may be the most appropriate first goal for beginning therapists as it will lend credibility to your training and help you build your practice. Therapist candidates can earn BCIA certification concurrently with training, and they offer the option of taking courses on a part-time basis.

ADVANCEMENT

Advancement opportunities are dependent on the main specialty a therapist has chosen and the environment in which he or she is working. Continuing education is important to any health care professional, so biofeedback therapists advance within their practices by developing their skills and learning about new methods of treatment. In some cases, such as academic medical centers, the addition of biofeedback therapy to a practice may assist the therapist in reaching promotion goals.

EARNINGS

Biofeedback therapists generally charge from $50 to $150 per session. Depending on the level of their experience, the size of their client base, and their level of training, biofeedback therapists can have substantial earnings. Because biofeedback therapists come from different professional backgrounds, however, it is difficult to give a salary range for them as a group. For example, a clinical psychologist with a Ph.D. is going to make more money practicing biofeedback than will a social worker with a master's degree. Therapists working in more urban areas generally make more money than those in smaller communities. A therapist just starting out may have annual earnings in the $30,000s. More established therapists, even in rural areas, may make around $50,000, while those working in larger communities, often handling many patients, may make up to $200,000 a year.

WORK ENVIRONMENT

Biofeedback therapists typically spend much of their time working one-on-one with patients. As with most health care practices, they may work in any number of environments, from solo private practices to larger medical centers or corporate complexes. Their responsibilities run the gamut from one-on-one patient visits to collaborative efforts with physicians and diagnosticians tackling difficult cases. Therapists primarily work in an office, although the increasing portability of computers means this may eventually change as well, allowing biofeedback practitioners even to consider house calls on a regular basis.

OUTLOOK

The employment outlook for biofeedback therapists is good. According to the U.S. Department of Labor, overall employment in health care will grow much faster than the average for all industries through 2014. While the department does not provide specific projections for biofeedback therapists, it is logical to conclude they will be in demand for several reasons. One reason is the growing population of Americans aged 65 and over. People in this age group are more likely to need and seek out treatments for many different conditions. This will increase the demand for most health care industry workers, including biofeedback therapists. Also, because most individuals have some sort of medical insurance, the costs of care, including nontraditional courses of treatment such as biofeedback therapy, have become more affordable. According to EEG Spectrum International, many insurance plans cover biofeedback therapy for treatment of certain conditions.

In many cases, patients seek the assistance of biofeedback therapists after more traditional medical treatment has failed. On the other hand, some people choose to look first to alternative forms of health care to avoid medications or invasive surgery.

In addition, continued research within the field of biofeedback should allow for the treatment of more disorders. Subspecialties like neurobiofeedback are increasing dramatically. The study of brain waves in cases involving alcoholism, attention deficit disorder, insomnia, epilepsy, and traumatic brain injury point to new biofeedback treatment methods.

Some conditions, such as chronic headaches, are often better treated through biofeedback therapy than through more invasive medical treatment.

FOR MORE INFORMATION

The AAPB is dedicated to the promotion of biofeedback as a means of improving health. Its Web site is a good place to begin to gather more information about the field.

Association for Applied Psychophysiology and Biofeedback (AAPB)
10200 West 44th Avenue, Suite 304
Wheat Ridge, CO 80033-2840
Tel: 303-422-8436
Email: AAPB@resourcenter.com
http://www.aapb.org

For more information about biofeedback, certification, and approved programs, contact
Biofeedback Certification Institute of America
10200 West 44th Avenue, Suite 310
Wheat Ridge, CO 80033-2840
Tel: 303-420-2902
Email: bcia@resourcenter.com
http://www.bcia.org

For more on neurofeedback, including research, news, and practitioners, contact
EEG Spectrum International Inc.
21601 Vanowen Street, Suite 100
Canoga Park, CA 91303-2752
Tel: 818-789-3456
Email: info@eegspectrum.com
http://www.eegspectrum.com

Child Life Specialists

OVERVIEW

Child life specialists work in health care settings to help infants, children, adolescents, and their families through illness or injury. One of the primary roles of the child life specialist is to ease the anxiety and stress that often accompany hospitalization, injury, or routine medical care. Child life specialists help children, adolescents, and their families maintain living patterns that are as close to normal as possible, and they try to minimize the potential trauma of hospitalization. Child life specialists do this by providing opportunities for play and relaxation, interaction with other children, and personalized attention. They also encourage family involvement, which can play a major role in helping children and adolescents cope with difficult situations. Child life specialists may help children and their families to develop coping skills and educate them about the experience that they are going through.

Some hospitals refer to their child life specialists as *play therapists, patient activity therapists, activity therapists,* or *therapeutic recreation specialists.*

QUICK FACTS

School Subjects
Health
Psychology

Personal Skills
Communication/ideas
Helping/teaching

Work Environment
Primarily indoors
Primarily one location

Minimum Education Level
Bachelor's degree

Salary Range
$34,864 to $42,000 to $49,098+

Certification or Licensing
Recommended

Outlook
About as fast as the average

DOT
195

GOE
12.02.02

NOC
N/A

O*NET-SOC
21-1021.00

HISTORY

At one time physicians and nurses were the only adults responsible for the care of children in hospitals. Parents left their children in hospitals, frequently for long periods of time, for treatment of their illnesses. But many parents felt that their children's emotional needs were not being met. Children were often not told about what tests, treatments, or procedures they were to undergo, and as a result their hospital experience was frequently traumatic. In addition, social

A child life specialist works with a sick child at a hospital. *(Bob Daemmrich, The Image Works)*

workers who were part of the health care team sometimes were not specially trained to work with children and could not provide them with support.

During the early 20th century, attempts were made to improve health care workers' understanding of children's needs and to make hospital stays less emotionally difficult for children. C. S. Mott Hospital in Ann Arbor, Michigan, for example, created the nation's first child life department, focusing on child development, in 1922. Gradually, during the 1940s and 1950s, "play programs" were developed at various care facilities across the country. In these settings children were allowed to relax, play, and feel safe. As professional interest in and understanding of child development grew, the play programs began to be seen not only as a play time but also as a therapeutic part of children's care during hospital stays. During the 1960s and 1970s the field of child life grew dramatically as it gained increasing acceptance.

The profession of child life specialist was formally recognized in 1974, when the Association for the Care of Children's Health formed a committee for child life and activity specialists. The committee, which became the independent organization Child Life Council (CLC) in 1982, had as its goals to promote the profession of child life specialist as well as to strengthen these specialists' professional identity. The committee's members recognized that the interruption of a hospitalization or even an ambulatory procedure could have negative consequences for children's growth and development. Today, child life specialists are recognized as an integral part of a child's health care team.

THE JOB

When children are hospitalized, the experience can be frightening. Child life specialists need to be tuned into the child or adolescent's concerns. For some children, separation from their families and the familiarity of home can be traumatic. For others, repeated blood tests, needles, or painful procedures can cause fears or nightmares. Emotional damage can be a danger even for adolescents. No matter how short or long the hospital stay and no matter how serious the illness or injury, children can experience anxiety or other emotional effects.

Child life specialists try to ease the possible trauma of being in the hospital. They play an important role in educating and comforting both the patients and their families. They become familiar and trusted adults, and they are usually the only professionals who do not perform tests on the children.

Child life specialists may use dolls and medical instruments to show children what the doctor will be doing. They may help children act out their concerns by having them give a doll a shot if they receive one. The child life specialist may use recreational activities, art projects, cooking, music, and outdoor play in their work. Programs are tailored to meet the needs of individual patients. Some children are unable to express their fears and concerns and may need the child life specialist to draw them out. Some children rely on the child life specialist to help them understand what is happening to them. Still others need the child life specialist to explain children's emotional outbursts or withdrawal to their families.

When children are hospitalized for a long period of time, child life specialists may accompany them to procedures, celebrate successful treatment, or plan a holiday celebration. Child life specialists may also take children on preadmission orientation and hospital tours. They serve as advocates for children's issues by promoting rooming-in or unrestricted parental or sibling visits. Many child life specialists work in conjunction with local school districts to help children keep up with school while they are in the hospital.

Child life administrators supervise the staffs of child life personnel. In larger hospitals, the administrators work with other hospital administrators to run the child life programs smoothly within the hospital setting.

Child life specialists can turn their patients' hospital stays into a time of growth. Children are very resilient, and with proper care by their entire health team, they can emerge from hospital stays with a sense of accomplishment and heightened self-esteem.

REQUIREMENTS

High School

If you are interested in becoming a child life specialist, you will need to plan on going to college after high school. Therefore, you should take a college preparatory curriculum. As a child life specialist you will need to understand family dynamics, child development, educational play, and basic medical terminology. To help you prepare for this specialty, take psychology and sociology courses and, if available, child development classes. In addition, be sure that your class schedule includes science courses, including health and biology. Because communication is such an important aspect of this work, take English, communication, and speech classes. You may also want to take art, physical education, and drama classes to develop skills that you can use in a variety of therapies, such as play, art, and recreation therapy.

Postsecondary Training

Some colleges or universities offer specific programs in child life, and quite a number of schools offer course work in areas related to child life. Those who attend colleges or universities that do not have specific child life programs should major in another appropriate field, such as child development, psychology, and social work. Do some research before you select a school to attend. The CLC advises those considering this career to look for a school program that has sufficient faculty, a variety of field opportunities, and positive student evaluations. The CLC offers the *Directory of Child Life Programs*, which has information on both undergraduate and graduate programs. Typical classes to take include child psychology, child growth and development, family dynamics, and theories of play. Select a program that offers internships. An internship will give you supervised experience in the field as well as prepare you for future employment.

A child life administrator is usually required to have a master's degree in child development, behavioral psychology, education, or a related field. Graduate-level course work typically includes the areas of administration, research, and advanced clinical issues. Those who wish to be considered for positions as child life administrators must also have work experience supervising staff members, managing budgets, and preparing educational materials.

Certification or Licensing

Certification as a certified child life specialist is available through the CLC's Child Life Certifying Committee. Certification criteria include having a bachelor's degree, passing an examination, completing 480 hours of a child life internship or fellowship, and having a minimum of 4,000 hours of paid clinical child life experience. Although certification is voluntary, it is highly recommended. Some health care centers will not hire a child life specialist who is not certified.

Other Requirements

To be a successful child life specialist you should enjoy working with people, especially children. You will be part of a health care team, so you must be able to communicate effectively with medical professionals as well as able to communicate with children and their families. You must be creative in order to come up with different ways to explain complicated events, such as a surgery, to a child without frightening him or her. You will also need maturity and emotional stability to deal with situations that may otherwise upset you, such as seeing chronically ill or severely injured children. Those who enjoy this work are able to focus on its positive aspects—helping children and their families through difficult times.

EXPLORING

An excellent way to explore your interest in and aptitude for this work is to volunteer. For volunteer opportunities in medical settings, find out what local hospitals, outpatient clinics, or nursing homes have to offer. Opportunities to work with children are also available through organizations such as Easter Seals, Boy Scouts and Girl Scouts, and Big Brothers/Big Sisters of America. In addition, volunteer or paid positions are available at many summer camps. Babysitting, of course, is another way to work with children as well as earn extra money. And a good babysitter is always in demand, no matter where you live.

Once you are in college you can join the CLC as a student member. Membership includes a subscription to the council's newsletter, which can give you a better understanding of the work of a child life specialist.

EMPLOYERS

Child life specialists work as members of the health care team typically in hospitals. Increasingly, though, specialists are finding employment outside of hospitals at such places as rehabilitation centers, hospices, and ambulatory care facilities. Most child life programs in hospitals are autonomous and report to hospital administrations as other departments and programs do.

Child life programs often work with school programs within hospitals. Specialists may work with teachers to coordinate the curriculum with recreational activities. They also may encourage hospital administrations to provide adequate classroom facilities and highly qualified teachers.

STARTING OUT

Your internship may provide you with valuable contacts that can give you information on job leads. In addition, the career services office of your college or university should be able to help you locate your first job. The CLC offers its members use of a job bank that lists openings at hospitals and clinics. You may also contact the human resources departments of hospitals directly for information on available positions.

ADVANCEMENT

Becoming certified and keeping up with new developments through continuing education workshops and seminars are the first two steps anyone must take in order to advance in this field. The next step is to get a graduate degree. Advancement possibilities include the positions of child life administrator, assistant director, or director of a child life program. Advanced positions involve management responsibilities, including the overseeing of a staff and coordinating a program's activities. Those in advanced positions must also keep their knowledge up to date by completing continuing education, attending professional conferences, and reading professional journals.

EARNINGS

Salaries for child life specialists vary greatly depending on such factors as the region of the country a specialist works in, education level, certification, and the size of the employer. For example, salaries tend to be higher in large metropolitan teaching hospitals than in small community hospitals. According to Salary.com, salaries for child life specialists ranged from $34,864 to $49,098 or more in 2007. The median income for workers in the field was approximately $42,000. Those with the highest earnings are usually child life administrators or directors. In addition, child life specialists with certification tend to earn more than their noncertified counterparts.

Benefits vary by employer, but they usually include such items as paid vacation and sick days, medical insurance, and retirement plans.

WORK ENVIRONMENT

Child life specialists are members of the health care team in a variety of settings, including hospitals, clinics, and hospice facilities. In most hospitals, the child life specialist works in a special playroom. Sometimes the specialist may go to the child's hospital room. In outpatient facilities, the specialist may work in a waiting room or a designated playroom. According to the American Academy of Pediatrics (AAP), the ratio of child life specialists to children that works well is about one to 15. Child life specialists must be comfortable in hospital settings. They need to adjust easily to being around children who are sick. Since the children and their families need so much support, child life specialists need to be emotionally stable. Their own support network of family and friends should be strong, so that the specialist can get through difficult times at work. Child life specialists may have patients who die, and this can be difficult.

Most child life personnel work during regular business hours, although specialists are occasionally needed on evenings, holidays, or weekends to work with children. It is important for child life personnel to have hobbies or outside interests to avoid becoming too emotionally drained from the work. The rewards of a child life specialist career are great. Many child life specialists see the direct effects of their work on their patients and on their patients' families. They see anxiety and fear being eased, and they see their patients come through treatments and hospitalizations with a renewed pride.

OUTLOOK

The employment outlook for child life specialists is good. The AAP reports that most hospitals specializing in pediatric care have child life programs. In addition, the number of these programs has doubled since 1965. And although managed-care providers encourage short hospital stays that may result in a reduced need for staffing in hospitals, opportunities for child life specialists are increasing outside of the hospital setting. The possible employers of today and tomorrow include outpatient clinics, rehabilitation centers, hospice programs, and other facilities that may treat children, such as sexual assault centers and centers for abused women and children.

FOR MORE INFORMATION

For current news on issues affecting children's health, visit the AAP's Web site.

American Academy of Pediatrics (AAP)
141 Northwest Point Boulevard
Elk Grove Village, IL 60007-1098
Tel: 847-434-4000
Email: pedscareer@aap.org
http://www.aap.org

For education, career, and certification information as well as professional publications, contact

Child Life Council
11820 Parklawn Drive, Suite 240
Rockville, MD 20852-2529
Tel: 301-881-7090
Email: clcstaff@childlife.org
http://www.childlife.org

For information on children's health issues and pediatric care, contact

National Association of Children's Hospitals and Related Institutions
401 Wythe Street
Alexandria, VA 22314-1927
Tel: 703-684-1355
http://www.childrenshospitals.net

Grief Therapists

OVERVIEW

A *grief therapist* or *bereavement counselor* offers therapy for those who are mourning the death of a family member or a loved one. Therapists help survivors work through possible feelings of anger or guilt and help them recover from their loss. Counselors may be brought into communities or facilities to help individuals after a national disaster, act of violence, or an accident. Grief therapists may be self-employed as independent counselors or work for hospitals, funeral homes, schools, hospice organizations, nursing homes, or government or private agencies.

HISTORY

Grief therapy is a relatively new career specialty. According to Dr. Dana Cable, professor of psychology and thanatology at Hood College in Frederick, Maryland, and a certified grief therapist and death educator, "Grief therapy is a growing area because of the nature of many deaths today. There are many more issues to be worked through when we lose young people to violent deaths and diseases such as AIDS. In addition, there is some movement away from organized religion where people used to find comfort when they lost a loved one." Cable also points out that changes in the family unit have affected the way in which family members grieve. Many families are not close, physically or emotionally, resulting in issues of guilt when a family member dies. Other factors that have boosted growth in this field include people's willingness to accept the help of a therapist (something that rarely happened in years past) and the large number of aging baby boomers who are now beginning to experience the

QUICK FACTS

School Subjects
Psychology
Sociology

Personal Skills
Communication/ideas
Helping/teaching

Work Environment
Primarily indoors
Primarily one location

Minimum Education Level
Master's degree

Salary Range
$21,890 to $34,380 to $59,700+

Certification or Licensing
Voluntary (certification)
Required by certain states (licensing)

Outlook
Faster than the average

DOT
195

GOE
12.02.02

NOC
4153

O*NET-SOC
19-3031.03, 21-1014.00

deaths of friends and family members and, thus, have a need for grief therapists' services.

THE JOB

Grief therapists help individuals accept the death of a spouse, child, partner, parent, sibling, or loved one. Therapists give their clients reassurance and help them examine and resolve feelings, including negative ones, that may be associated with the death. Counseling may be done on a one-to-one basis, with a small group, or as part of a support group.

When disasters such as accidents or violence occur, grief therapists are often brought in to speak to communities, schools, or organizations. They help people deal with the tragedy and may provide individual counseling. In recent times, therapists have been called upon when violence has hit schools, when weather-related tragedies have destroyed communities, and when an airplane has crashed or a terrorist bombing has occurred.

Hospitals, nursing homes, AIDS and cancer care centers, and hospice organizations employ grief therapists to provide emotional support to patients and their families and friends. In addition, some funeral homes refer families and friends to grief therapists as part of an aftercare service following a funeral.

Grief therapists also work as *death educators*. These specialists conduct classes for people who work in professions that deal with the sick and dying, such as medical and nursing students. They may also speak to organizations, clubs, support groups, parents, and others about issues related to death and give them suggestions on how to cope.

REQUIREMENTS

High School

College prep classes are essential if you wish to enter the field of grief therapy. In order to learn how to deal with a diverse group of people from all cultural backgrounds, courses in health, sociology, psychology, and religion are helpful. Communication is a key part of the grief therapist's job, so speech, foreign languages, communication, and English courses are also vital. It may be a good idea to check with the colleges you have selected to find out what courses they recommend for a career in psychology and counseling.

Postsecondary Training

Degrees that feature a strong psychology component or a pre-med program are usually recommended for counselors. This must be followed with a master's program in counseling, social work, or psychology. Following this with a doctoral degree in psychology is recommended for the best job prospects.

Certification and Licensing

The Association for Death Education and Counseling offers the certification in thanatology and the fellow in thanatology designations to applicants who meet educational and experiential requirements and pass a multiple-choice examination. Certification must be renewed every three years.

Some states require grief therapists to obtain licenses in order to practice. These licensing requirements may vary from state to state, so it is best to check with the state in which you plan to practice. The American Counseling Association also offers detailed information on state licensing requirements for counselors. (See For More Information at the end of this article.) Some states may limit counselors' private practices to areas in which they have developed professional competence. There may also be some continuing education requirements for license renewal.

Other Requirements

If you are interested in becoming a grief therapist, you should enjoy working with people and feel comfortable dealing with clients who have suffered personal loss. You should show patience and be a compassionate listener, as well as be able to express yourself clearly and tactfully.

Grief therapists must not let their jobs take an emotional toll on their own lives. Though they hear many stories of grief and sadness, therapists can also find their job rewarding and uplifting as they help people overcome feelings of depression and despair and continue with their lives.

EXPLORING

Your high school guidance counselor may be able to supply information on a career as a therapist. Other sources for information can be found at your local or school library, or through the Internet. Contact the organizations listed at the end of this article for further information.

Doing volunteer work for organizations such as the Red Cross or with your local hospital, nursing home, or hospice care center will give you more experience dealing with the sick, troubled, or grieving. Participating in high school clubs or other groups that organize volunteer projects to benefit homeless people, victims of AIDS, or battered spouses can also give you valuable experience.

EMPLOYERS

Grief therapists may provide grief therapy as an independent part of their larger counseling practice, or they may work as part of an organization. Many therapists in private practice offer grief therapy. Some therapists are part of a group practice of medical or psychological professionals who offer a variety of counseling and therapy services. Funeral homes, nursing homes, assisted care facilities, AIDS care facilities, hospice organizations, and almost any facility or organization that deals with the sick and dying use grief therapists. Many have a therapist either on call or on staff. The government may also employ counselors and grief therapists in their health care facilities.

Some grief therapists may work under contract with large corporations as part of employee assistance programs. Others may be called upon by airlines, schools, communities, or businesses at times of crisis or when violence has occurred. They may also work on a contract basis to make presentations or conduct seminars to various groups or organizations.

Grief therapists may also work at colleges or universities, conducting research or teaching classes that deal with death and grief.

STARTING OUT

Some colleges and universities offer job placement for people seeking careers in counseling. While in graduate school, therapy students often work as interns with hospitals, hospices, health care, or crisis care organizations, or with therapists in private practices. These relationships can often offer employment and networking possibilities after graduation.

Most grief therapists practice general counseling before specializing in grief therapy. Building a client base as a counselor can help provide the base for beginning a career in grief therapy. Personal contacts can also provide networking possibilities. Membership in a professional counseling association may offer sources for contacts and help you find job leads. Classified advertisements and trade magazines also list job openings.

ADVANCEMENT

Counselors specializing in grief therapy can advance to head their own counseling service or group practice, serving clients directly or contracting out services to hospitals, businesses, hospice organizations, and other facilities. Experienced grief therapists who specialize in education can become department heads of universities or colleges. Counselors with a business background and experience can advance to become executive directors of health care facilities, organizations, nursing homes, or head professional organizations that serve the counseling profession.

EARNINGS

The salary range for grief therapists is generally the same as for other therapists and counselors. According to the U.S. Department of Labor, the median annual salary of mental health counselors was $34,380 in 2006. The lowest paid 10 percent earned less than $21,890, and the highest paid 10 percent earned more than $59,700. Therapists in private practice and those who become directors of facilities may earn considerably more.

Benefits vary depending on the position and the employer but generally vacation, sick leave, insurance, and other work-related benefits are provided. Persons who are self-employed usually have to provide their own insurance and retirement funds.

WORK ENVIRONMENT

Generally, grief therapists work in office settings that are clean and well lighted. Grief therapists who work in crisis situations will find a wide variety of working environments depending on the situation, but usually small, temporary offices are set up to accommodate counselors.

Counselors in private or group practice may have to set up evening and weekend office hours. Some grief counseling must be done on an emergency basis in times of crisis or violence, so there may be occasions when counselors have to drop everything to work any time of the day or night.

Many counselors stick to a given location to serve the local community. However, depending on the type and range of cases the therapist handles, travel may be necessary, including on nights and weekends.

OUTLOOK

According to the *Occupational Outlook Handbook*, employment opportunities in counseling are expected to grow faster than the average for all occupations through 2014. Demand should be strongest for counselors concentrating on rehabilitation and on mental health, which includes grief therapy.

A career in grief therapy holds great promise. Our changing and aging society creates a need for grief counseling. As baby boomers age and experience the deaths of their parents, friends, and families, they are seeking the help of bereavement counselors to help them adjust and deal with their feelings. Counseling has become a socially accepted tool to help people deal with difficult or painful situations.

As violent crimes occur and as young people witness acts of violence and experience the untimely death of friends, they seek an understanding that grief counselors can help provide. Car accidents, AIDS, and drug-related deaths can also create feelings of guilt and depression that counselors can help people work through. Unfortunately, there will continue to be natural disasters such as tornadoes, floods, avalanches, and earthquakes that kill large numbers of people. Grief counselors will continue to be called on to help ease survivors' pain.

Although grief therapists work in every part of the country, demand is highest in retirement areas of the country where there is a large elderly population.

FOR MORE INFORMATION

For information on state licensing, certification, accredited graduate programs, and choosing a graduate program, contact
American Counseling Association
5999 Stevenson Avenue
Alexandria, VA 22304-3304
Tel: 800-347-6647
http://www.counseling.org

For career and certification information, contact
Association for Death Education and Counseling
60 Revere Drive, Suite 500
Northbrook, IL 60062-1591
Tel: 847-509-0403
http://www.adec.org

For information on working with grieving children and their families, contact
The Dougy Center
National Center for Grieving Children and Families
PO Box 86852
Portland, OR 97286-0852
Tel: 866-775-5683
Email: help@dougy.org
http://www.grievingchild.org

For information on working with the elderly, contact
Gerontological Society of America
1220 L Street, NW, Suite 901
Washington, DC 20005-4001

Tel: 202-842-1275
Email: geron@geron.org
http://www.geron.org

For information on graduate programs in thanatology, or the study of grief therapy, contact the following colleges

College of New Rochelle
Graduate School, Division of Human Services
29 Castle Place
New Rochelle, NY 10805-2330
Tel: 914-654-5561
Email: gs@cnr.edu
http://www.cnr.edu/ACADEMICS/gs/gs-thanatology.html

Hood College
401 Rosemont Avenue
Frederick, MD 21701-8575
Tel: 301-663-3131
http://www.hood.edu/academics/departments.
cfm?pid=departments_psychology.html

INTERVIEW

Dr. Jane Bissler is the clinical director of Counseling for Wellness, LLP in Kent, Ohio. She discussed her career and the field of grief counseling with the editors of Careers in Focus: Therapists.

Q. Please tell us about yourself and your practice.

A. I am a counselor, teacher, writer, and speaker. I'm a practicing clinical counselor and clinical director of Counseling for Wellness, LLP. I'm recognized as a fellow in thanotology by the Association of Death Education and Counseling (ADEC). I'm also an adjunct professor in the Community Counseling and Counselor Education and Supervision programs at Kent State University. I teach courses in bereavement, counseling, and assessments.

I'm currently a member of the board of directors for the Association of Death Education and Counseling and have belonged to this organization for 20 years. My clinical research and specialty focuses on what has been most helpful for parents who are grieving the death of their adolescent children. I have recently completed my first book, which is a collection of true spiritual events experienced by grievers. I write a weekly grief question and answer newspaper column, which is also carried on my Web site, http://www.counselingforloss.com. I have been writing this column since 1990 and receive questions from all over the world.

Q. Can you name a few things that young people may not know about a career in grief therapy?

A. To be a counselor, one must have an undergraduate degree in the field of their choice (usually psychology or social work) and have a graduate degree in counseling. They may also go on for a Ph.D. in counseling or counselor education and supervision. It is a minimum of six years of full-time college. Licensure requirements are stipulated by each state. Having a certificate in this specialty requires continuing studies and testing.

The educational process is very important and sometimes not clearly understood by those who wish to enter this field. Especially for a specialization area, such as bereavement, it is important that the counselor be educated with a broad base of mental health diagnosis, funeral/memorial customs, and the needs of the culture they are working with. Keeping abreast of the newest research being done in the field of thanotology will also benefit the counselor and the client. The vast majority of this research comes from those belonging to the ADEC. Having a strong membership in the premier professional organization in the specialty you are working in is of the utmost importance.

Having the need for being nonjudgmental and having great empathy for and about the grief process is also surprising for some who are thinking about going into this field. Everyone grieves differently and it is important to meet the clients where they are. The practices of some clients may seem weird or odd to the counselor, but it is a necessity for the counselor to embrace these if the counseling is to be helpful.

I think the one main surprising aspect for people interested in doing bereavement work is the need that they, themselves, have a balanced life. People who are grieving are incredibly sad and become isolated. Sometimes the counselor is their only understanding link to the outside world. Working with seven or eight grieving clients a day can be draining for the counselor. It's difficult to be sitting with someone who is feeling hopeless, who is trying to learn the new language of grief, who is working hard to assimilate the death of their loved one and still remain part of a world that wants them to "get over it" and return to what they believe is normal living. Having a balanced life means that the counselor will need to get plenty of rest, eat a nutritious diet, and exercise. The counselor also needs to have enough social outlets to see clearly the world their clients live in. Due to the absolute need for confidentiality in this profession, it is also important that the counselor find a way to network with other professionals so that the difficult cases can be discussed with another professional. Through this processing, the counselor will be able to leave work at work so he or she does not carry the client's grief home. It is very important for the bereavement counselor to have worked through his or her own grief issues. When the counselor is with a client, the client does not want to hear about the counselor's loss experiences. Many clients come to me after meeting with another counselor who either cried when the client was telling their story of loss or where the counselor told their own story of loss.

Q. Tell us about a day in your life on the job.

A. I see about 25 clients per week. Some days I only see four clients and other days I see eight. I usually arrive at my office an hour before my first client is scheduled to come in.

Before meeting with each client, I check their file to remind myself of the treatment plan and what we are scheduled to do during this session. I also read my previous progress notes to remind myself of what we talked about during our last sessions.

I greet each client in the waiting area and escort them back to my office. I meet with each client for 50 to 60 minutes. Although the treatment plan points the intended direction of the session, sometimes the issues the client has faced since last in my office take precedence over the scheduled treatment plan. At the conclusion of the session, a new appointment time is scheduled and the client is given a reminder card.

If I finish my session in 50 minutes, which is recommended, I type up my progress notes of that session, update the treatment plan, if needed, and record the occurrence of the session for billing purposes.

At the end of the day, I catch up on any progress notes and treatment plans missed, billing information, return phone calls, record their occurrences, and pull information to be used the next day by my clients. I will also note research that I need to do for the clients I saw that day. This takes about another 60 to 90 minutes.

Many counselors schedule several hours a week to do their paperwork and research for the next week's clients. It all depends on the client schedule and when you can find time to do this. I enjoy reading new material and doing online research on my front porch so I will often take the information home and read there instead of extending my time in the office.

Q. What are some of the pros and cons of your job?

A. The pros of being a counselor are numerous. Having the ability to walk with a client through a difficult, but extremely meaningful, time of life is truly a gift. Getting to know someone at this level is gratifying and unusual in today's faceless society.

When someone knows you are a counselor, there is a certain prestige associated with this title. Everyone has the need to talk to an uninvolved party and get a unique perspective. A counselor is a popular guest at parties! This happens so frequently that many of us do not tell people our true professions when on an airplane. Otherwise, the flight becomes a counseling session for your seatmate!

Being able to help someone is very important. Not only does counseling help others but it also helps our own soul's growth. It helps us have perspective, gain personal growth, and adds meaning to our own lives. The field of grief work helps us keep our own priorities in order and value the time we have with our friends and families.

The field of counseling is intellectually stimulating. You never really know what a client is going to say. Being able to pull on your vast knowledge and experiences keeps our memories sharp and our brains active.

There are also cons to being a counselor. The field of billing for services through insurance companies is tedious and many times fruitless. It's difficult to understand and follow the paper trail to get paid for the work we do. Having a good office administrator is the only way to financially make ends meet.

Some clients don't want to do the hard work needed to assimilate the loss of a loved one. They want the pain to dissolve and they want their lives back the way they were. While this is understandable, counselors are not needed for someone who does not want to find a way to find new footing for this new life. Also, some clients have other mental health problems. These are extremely complicated when a death happens. Grief counselors need to have a good knowledge and appreciation for all mental health issues. Even the mentally ill experience the death of loved ones!

The final con to being a grief counselor is the perception that most counselors face. Clients believe they need to be "nuts" to come to a counselor. This is definitely not the case, especially for someone who is grieving. Our clients certainly tell us that they feel out of control and unable to function. For them this is "nuts." We are constantly fighting this belief of society.

Q. What are the most important personal and professional qualities for grief counselors?

A. The most important personal and professional qualities for grief counselors are empathy, having an unconditional positive regard, being nonjudgmental, having an excellent memory, being able to conceptualize the life of your client, having a solid knowledge base of grief and loss information and research, being certified in the field, having untold patience with your clients, and having a strong professional identity through the best professional organizations, research, and literary publications. Finally, knowing the culture you are working in and the way it deals with grief.

Q. What advice would you give to young people who are interested in the field?

A. I wish there was some way for those interested in this field to shadow a counselor for a day. Unfortunately, due to the confidential nature of the counselor/client relationships this is not possible. However, I would suggest reading lay journals, such as *Living with Loss,* to see the writings of professionals from the field as well as grieving people.

I would also suggest doing an Internet search and looking at grief Web sites, such as http://www.counselingforloss.com. Again, the student would be able to see the professional as well as the griever's writings.

There are many excellent books, as well, that will give a student a window into the grieving mind and heart. You might want to read *Straight Talk About Death For Teenagers: How to Cope with Losing Someone You Love,* by Earl Grollman; *Creative Interventions in Grief and Loss Therapy: When the Music Stops, a Dream Dies,* edited by Thelma Duffey; *On Death and Dying,* by Elisabeth Kubler-Ross; and *What Helped Me When My Loved One Died,* by Earl Grollman.

If the student is grieving, attend a counselor-led grief group. Some groups are led by those who are grieving themselves, and attendance at these groups would not give you a glimpse into the counseling profession. Search for one led by a professional and watch how he or she leads, plans for, and manages the group.

Horticultural Therapists

OVERVIEW

Horticultural therapists combine their love of plants and nature with their desire to help people improve their lives. They use gardening, plant care, and other nature activities as therapy tools for helping their clients to feel better by doing such things as focusing on a project, improving social skills, and being physically active. In addition to these benefits, clients experience emotional benefits, such as feeling secure, responsible, and needed. Horticultural therapists' clients can include nursing home residents, psychiatric patients, prison inmates, "at risk" youth, and the mentally disabled. Frequently horticultural therapists work as part of a health care team, which may include doctors, physical therapists, nurses, social workers, and others.

HISTORY

Gardens have been grown for thousands of years, both for their beauty as well as their products. In the Middle Ages, for example, gardening took place mainly within the walls of monasteries, and gardens included herbs for medicinal purposes, flowers for the church, and fruits and vegetables for the monks to eat. In the United States, people also gardened for pleasure as well as practicality. With the opening of the Friends Asylum for the Insane in Pennsylvania in 1817, however, gardening and nature activities took on an additional purpose. The Friends Asylum, a hospital for the mentally ill, was built on a farm and had walkways, gardens, and tree-filled areas. As part of their treatment, patients were expected

School Subjects
Agriculture
Biology
Psychology

Personal Skills
Helping/teaching
Mechanical/manipulative

Work Environment
Indoors and outdoors
Primarily one location

Minimum Education Level
Bachelor's degree

Salary Range
$20,880 to $31,750 to
$55,530+

Certification or Licensing
Voluntary

Outlook
About as fast as the average

DOT
N/A

GOE
14.06.01

NOC
N/A

O*NET-SOC
29-1125.00

to participate in the upkeep of the grounds. In 1879, the Friends Asylum built a greenhouse for patient use and today is recognized as the first-known U.S. hospital to treat patients with what is now known as horticultural therapy.

The use of horticultural therapy did not become popular, however, until after World War II. Garden club groups, wanting to help wounded servicemen at veterans' hospitals, began volunteering and sharing their gardening know-how. By 1955, Michigan State University was the first university to award an undergraduate degree in horticultural therapy. Today horticultural therapists undergo special training, and a number of colleges and universities offer degrees or programs in horticultural therapy.

THE JOB

During an average workday, horticultural therapists usually spend much of their time working directly with clients. In addition to working with clients, horticultural therapists who hold management positions need to spend time managing staff, arranging schedules, and perhaps overseeing the work of volunteers. One of horticultural therapists' most important responsibilities is to assign the right task to each client so that their skills are enhanced and their confidence is boosted. After all, clients who are already depressed, for example, won't feel much better when the hard-to-grow plants that they were assigned to watch over suddenly die. In order to determine what projects will suit their clients, horticultural therapists begin by assessing each client's mental and physical state. This assessment may involve talking to the clients, reviewing medical records, and consulting with a physician or other health care professional about a treatment plan.

With the results from the assessment, therapists determine what kind of work will benefit the client. Therapists then assign the client a job. Therapists and clients may work in greenhouses, in outdoor garden areas on hospital grounds, in classroom-type settings to which the therapists have brought all the necessary supplies, or at community botanical gardens, to name a few locations. Depending on the work area, a client may be asked to put soil in cups to plant seeds, water a garden, or be part of a group activity in which something will be made from the garden's products, such as tea or dried flower arrangements. In some cases, the gardens' produce and plants are sold to help pay for expenses, such as the purchasing of new seeds and plants. In this way, clients may be involved in business goals and continue to develop their sense of accomplishment.

Establishing a place where clients can feel safe and useful is an important part of horticultural therapists' work. This may mean allowing clients to work at their own pace to complete a task, giving praise for accomplishments (no matter how small), encouraging clients to talk to each other to decrease feelings of loneliness, and ensuring that the atmosphere of the therapy session stays positive. Horticultural therapist Lorraine Hanson explains, "One of the benefits of this treatment is that patients get a chance to socialize with each other while they work. They look forward to that, and it helps them prepare to reenter their communities."

In addition to working with clients, horticultural therapists who are part of a health care team will likely need to spend some of their time attending meetings with other team members to report on a client's progress and discuss a continuing treatment plan. Horticultural therapists must also do some paperwork, keeping their own records about clients, projects that have been completed, and even expenses. A successful horticultural therapist must have creativity in order to think of new projects for clients to work on as well as figuring out how to tailor projects and tasks to meet the needs of each client.

Because horticultural therapists often work with clients who have profound or complex problems, such as people with Alzheimer's disease, they may be faced with situations in which the client doesn't improve or doesn't feel the therapy has been helpful. This can be frustrating and even discouraging for the therapist, but it is also an aspect of the job that each therapist needs to deal with.

Some horticultural therapists also provide consulting services, usually to architects, designers, and administrators of health care or human services facilities. For example, they may offer their professional advice during the building or redesigning of hospitals, schools, and assisted-living communities. They may help with landscaping, selecting plants that are suitable for the region and offer a variety of colors, shapes, and smells. They may advise on the creation of "barrier free" gardens that are accessible to those with disabilities. And, they may work on the design of interior spaces, such as greenhouses and solariums.

REQUIREMENTS

High School

You can begin to prepare for this career while you are still in high school. Science classes are important to take, including biology, chemistry, and earth science, which should all give you a basic understanding of growth processes. If your school offers agriculture classes, particularly those dealing with plants, be sure to take them. To learn about different groups of people and how to relate to them, take sociology and psychology classes. English classes will help you develop your communication skills, which are vital in this profession. Other important classes to take to prepare you for college and work include mathematics, economics, and computer science.

Postsecondary Training

Horticultural therapy has only fairly recently been recognized as a profession in this country (as you recall, the first undergraduate degree in the field was given in 1955), and routes to enter this field have not yet become firmly established. To become registered by the American Horticultural Therapy Association (AHTA), however, you will need at least some related educational experience. Those in the field recommend that anyone wanting to work as a horticultural therapist should have, at a minimum, a bachelor's degree. A number of colleges offer degrees in horticultural therapy or horticulture degrees with a concentration in horticultural therapy, including Kansas State University, Rutgers University, and the University of Maine–Orono. The AHTA provides a listing of schools offering these programs on its Web site, http://www.ahta.org. Course work generally includes studies in botany, plant pathology, soil science, psychology, group dynamics, counseling, communications, business management, and economics, to name a few areas. In addition, an internship involving direct work with clients is usually required. Other facilities, such as botanic gardens, may offer certificate programs, but, naturally, these programs are much smaller in scope than horticulture degree programs.

Certification or Licensing

The AHTA offers voluntary certification in the form of the horticultural therapist registered (HTR) designation. Applicants for the HTR credential must have a four-year college degree (with required course content in horticulture, human services, and horticultural therapy) and complete a 480-hour internship (field work) under the supervision of an AHTA-registered horticultural therapist. Currently no licensing exists for horticultural therapists.

Other Requirements

Horticultural therapists must have a strong desire to help people, enjoy working with diverse populations, and be able to see each client as an individual. Just as important, of course, horticultural therapists must have an interest in science, a love of nature, and a "green thumb." These therapists need to be creative, perceptive, and able to manage groups. They must be able to interact with a variety of professionals, such as doctors, social workers, administrators, and architects, and work well as part of a team. As therapists, they may develop close emotional relationships with their clients, but they also must stop themselves from becoming emotionally over involved and realize the limits of their responsibilities. This work can often be quite physical, involving lifting and carrying, outdoor work, and work with the hands, so horticultural therapists should be in good physical shape.

EXPLORING

There are a number of ways you can explore your interest in this field. No matter where you live, become involved in gardening. This may mean gardening in your own backyard, creating a window box garden, or working at a community garden. To increase your gardening knowledge, join gardening groups and read about gardening on Web sites such as those by the National Gardening Association and the Garden Club of America (see the end of this article for contact information). Such sites usually provide tips for gardeners as well as information on gardening events. Volunteer at a local public facility, such as a museum with a garden, a botanic garden, or a nature trail, to meet others interested in and knowledgeable about gardening. Keep up-to-date by reading gardening magazines and talking to professionals, such as greenhouse managers. You can also get a part-time or summer job at a gardening supply store, greenhouse, or even the floral section of a grocery store.

Of course, it is just as important to explore your interest in working with people who need some type of assistance. Therefore, get paid part-time or summer work at a nursing home, hospital, assisted-care facility, or even a day care center. If you are unable to find paid work, get experience by volunteering at one of these places.

EMPLOYERS

Hospitals, rehabilitation centers, botanical centers, government social service agencies, and prisons are among the institutions that may employ horticultural therapists. In addition, horticultural therapists may work independently as consultants.

STARTING OUT

An internship completed during your college years provides an excellent way to make contacts with professionals in the field. These contacts may be able to help you find a job once you graduate. Also, by joining the AHTA, you will be able to network with other professionals and find out about job openings. Your school's career services office may be able to provide you with information about employers looking to hire horticultural therapists. You can also apply directly to facilities such as hospitals, nursing homes, and botanical centers.

ADVANCEMENT

Advancement in this profession typically comes with increased education and experience. Horticultural therapists may advance by becoming registered at the HTM level, moving into management positions, and overseeing the work of other therapists on staff. Some may advance by adding consulting to their current responsibilities. Others may consider it an advancement to move into consulting full time. Still others may move into teaching at schools offering horticultural therapy programs.

EARNINGS

The U.S. Department of Labor reports that the median annual earnings of recreational therapists were $34,990 in 2006. Salaries ranged from less than $20,880 to more than $55,530 a year. Rehabilitation counselors had median annual earnings of $29,200 and mental health counselors had median earnings of $34,380.

According to the most recent AHTA survey available, beginning horticulture therapists make approximately $25,315. Those with five to 10 years of experience have annual earnings of approximately $31,750, and those with more than 10 years of experience earn approximately $36,295.

Benefits will depend on the employer but generally include standard ones, such as paid vacation and sick days and health insurance. Those who work as independent consultants will need to provide for their own health insurance and other benefits.

WORK ENVIRONMENT

Horticultural therapists work in many different environments. Big city community gardens, classrooms, greenhouses, and hospital psychiatric wards are just a few of the settings. Work environments, therefore, can include being outdoors in the sun all day; being in a locked facility, such as for psychiatric patients or prisoners; being in warm, stuffy greenhouses; and being in an air-conditioned school. No matter where horticultural therapists work, though, they are in the business of helping people, and they spend most of their day interacting with others, such as clients, doctors, and volunteers. Because the therapists try to create calm, safe environments for their clients, the environments the therapists spend much of their time working in will be calm as well. Horticultural therapists shouldn't mind getting a bit dirty during the course of the day; after all, they may need to demonstrate activities such as planting a row of seeds in wet soil.

OUTLOOK

The outlook for horticultural therapists is good. The U.S. Department of Labor reports that counselors will have faster-than-average employment growth, while recreational therapists will have slower-than-average employment growth. As horticultural therapy gains recognition both from professionals and the public, the demand for it is likely to increase.

One factor that may affect the availability of full-time jobs in hospitals is the cost-cutting measures used by managed care and other insurance companies to severely limit patients' hospital stays. However, this may create more opportunities for those working at outpatient centers and other facilities.

FOR MORE INFORMATION

For more information on the career, schools with horticultural therapy programs, registration, and publications, contact

American Horticultural Therapy Association
201 East Main Street, Suite 1405
Lexington, KY 40507-2004
Tel: 800-634-1603
http://www.ahta.org

To learn more about gardening, contact the following associations:

American Community Gardening Association
1777 East Broad Street
Columbus, OH 43203-2040
Tel: 877-275-2242
Email: info@communitygarden.org
http://www.communitygarden.org

Garden Club of America
14 East 60th Street, 3rd Floor
New York, NY 10022-7147
Tel: 212-753-8287
Email: info@gcamerica.org
http://www.gcamerica.org

National Gardening Association
1100 Dorset Street
South Burlington, VT 05403-8000
Tel: 802-863-5251
http://www.garden.org

Hypnotherapists

OVERVIEW

Hypnosis is a sleep-like state brought on by another person's suggestions. People under hypnosis may be suggested to relax, change their way of thinking, or even move under direction. *Hypnotherapists* help people use the powers of their minds to increase motivation, change behavior, and promote healing.

HISTORY

Hypnosis has been a phenomenon for thousands of years; shamans, healers, and medicine men and women of ancient tribes used trance and other states of consciousness to heal sickness and appease their gods. Some of today's professional hypnotherapists suggest that hypnotherapy began with these ancient healers.

The first recorded instance of hypnosis in modern times occurred in the 1700s, when Austrian physician Franz Mesmer touted the healing potential of the trance state in his patients. Mesmer had a very flamboyant hypnotic style, and he claimed considerable success in helping his patients to heal. This trance state became know as "mesmerism," in honor of this early practitioner.

Mesmerism continued to be used in Europe in the mid-1800s, albeit sparingly and with little encouragement from the established medical community. Records indicate that Scottish surgeon James Esdaile used mesmerism as the sole anesthetic during surgery, and John Elliotson, a British surgeon, had similar success in pain management. English physician James Braid coined the word *hypnosis* in the late 1800s, using the Greek word for sleep, *hypnos*.

In the years that followed, a number of French physicians began to investigate hypnosis more earnestly. Jean Martin Charcot determined that hypnosis was an abnormal, unsafe state. However, French physicians August Ambrose Liébeault and Hippolyte Bernheim actually considered hypnosis to be a very normal state of mind that was largely untapped. They did more research into the idea of suggestibility during the hypnotic state. Gradually, hypnosis became more accepted in wider circles.

In the early 1900s, Sigmund Freud also began to investigate hypnosis to explore his patients' psyches, but he eventually rejected it in favor of dream analysis and psychoanalysis. Freud's early rejection of hypnotherapy caused many in the medical establishment to lose interest in the field until the 1950s, when hypnosis regained popularity. The establishment of the National Guild of Hypnotists in 1951 helped bring solidarity and credibility to the profession.

In the 1960s and 1970s, hypnotherapy became a popular alternative therapy in the United States and the United Kingdom. Today, hypnotherapy is gaining more acceptance in the mainstream, although it may never reach the level of acceptance of more traditional therapies.

THE JOB

"You are getting very sleepy. When I snap my fingers, you will begin yodeling. After you awaken, you will cluck like a chicken every time the phone rings." Is this hypnotism? Perhaps, but the hypnotist acts of magic shows and clubs have little in common with certified hypnotherapy.

Hypnotherapists induce a hypnotic state in others in order to bring about a desired effect, such as increasing motivation or changing a behavior. They may also train people in self-hypnosis techniques. Hypnotherapists don't cast a spell, gain control of a person's mind, or do anything else that's magical or strange. Instead, they use hypnosis to help people tap the power of their own minds to help themselves.

Hypnosis has been proven to work in hundreds of ways, from helping people stop smoking to easing the pain of childbirth. Although hypnosis has been studied for centuries, exactly what makes hypnosis work is still being explored.

A hypnotic state is a sleep-like condition in which the brain waves have slowed and the client is much more relaxed than normal. He or she is not asleep, but aware of and sensitive to the surroundings. But where a fully alert mind might normally break in and stop the acceptance of a suggestion, the brain appears to accept ideas more readily under hypnosis.

Clients are always in control in the hypnotic state—they won't do or say anything that they wouldn't normally do or say. "It's a myth that you can get someone to do something against their morals or ethics," stresses Dr. Dwight F. Damon, president of the National Guild of Hypnotists (NGH).

Founded in 1951, the NGH is one of the oldest and largest organizations for hypnotherapists worldwide, with chapters in cities across the United States and Canada. Damon adds, "I could tell you, 'Go stand on your head in the corner,' and if you wouldn't do it normally if I suggested it, you wouldn't do it under hypnosis."

A typical session with a hypnotherapist takes place in an office or quiet room. The hypnotherapist begins by discussing with the clients what goals and expectations they may have. Does she want to quit biting her nails so she looks good for her wedding? Does he hope to overcome a fear of flying so he can visit his elderly grandfather in Europe? Does the couple want to stop smoking and eat a more healthy diet so they can set a good example for their children? Whatever the reason, hypnotherapists need to know why the client wants to accomplish his or her goal.

Most hypnotherapists also try to find out about the health, background, and lifestyle of their clients. "Then we explain to the patient what hypnosis is—or really, what hypnosis is not, because people have a lot of misconceptions about it," says Damon. "They think it's sleep, or that they're going to reveal some deep dark secret, or that someone's going to get control over their mind. But none of this is true."

Next, the hypnotherapist does conditioning or susceptibility tests, which check to see how open to suggestion the client is and which hypnosis techniques are likely to work best. For example, the hypnotherapist could have a client look steadily at an object while he or she talks in a monotone. Sounds like ocean waves, a ticking clock, or an air conditioner may help a client relax and focus. "I might have you look at a spot on the wall and say to you, 'Your eyelids are getting heavy, drowsy, tired . . . but do not close your eyes yet; look at the spot on the wall. Your eyelids are getting heavy, drowsy, tired . . . but do not close your eyes yet; look at the spot on the wall,'" Damon says. Guided by these suggestions, the client becomes more and more relaxed, drifting into a hypnotic state.

Under hypnosis, the client's attention is very concentrated on the hypnotherapist's voice. If a suggestion is made that the client accepts, such as, "You want to quit smoking," his or her mind will be highly responsive to the suggestion and accept it. "How long the process takes depends on what you're doing, but you usually don't need a lot of time," says Damon. One of the phenomena of hypnosis is that subjects often think they've been "under" for a shorter time than they actually have. "People may think they've been hypnotized for a few minutes, when actually it was 20 minutes," he says.

Sometimes it takes a few sessions before hypnosis works, that is, before the hypnotherapist is able to help clients enter a hypnotic state.

Hypnosis is also used in medical or clinical settings, and even in emergency situations. "Many of our people are training EMTs [emergency medical technicians] and paramedics in hypnosis," adds Damon. These workers may use hypnosis to help people under their care slow down the flow of blood, control breathing, and reduce pain and anxiety through positive suggestions.

Hypnosis is also helpful to mental health professionals. In the hypnotic state, a person may be more open to remembering past events that have affected them traumatically. Once these are remembered, a psychologist or other mental health professional can help the patient deal with them through therapy. Hypnotherapy can also help people replace negative thoughts with positive ones or deal with their fears.

Hypnosis has been used in the treatment of depression, schizophrenia, sleep disorders, anorexia, panic attacks, neuroses, attention deficit disorder, asthma, allergies, heart disease, headaches, arthritis, colon and bowel problems, and more. Experimental research is testing its use with cancer. Young children, for example, have been taught to picture good white blood cells eating cancer cells like the Pac-Man video game.

REQUIREMENTS

High School

If you're planning to make hypnotherapy your career, take a college-preparatory course of study in high school. Courses in health, biology, anatomy, and chemistry will give you a better understanding of the mind-body connection that is key to hypnotherapy. You may wish to study speech, communications, psychology, and sociology as well to help you learn to deal with clients and approach their treatments in the most effective manner.

You may prefer to use hypnosis as part of another career. If this is the case, you should do course work pertaining to your future field, for example, if you plan to use hypnotherapy in a dental practice. Advanced science and math classes in high school will prepare you for college, medical school, and beyond.

Postsecondary Training

If you wish to work only as a hypnotherapist (not combining hypnotherapy with the practices of another profession), you do not need a four-year college degree. You will, however, need some postsecondary training. Many schools across the country offer training in hypnosis, but it will be a key factor in your future success to attend a respected and accredited program. Look for a school or program that has been accredited by a professional organization, such as the American Council of Hypnotist Examiners (ACHE) or the NGH, as well as approved by the state's department of education. If you attend a program without these credentials, you will have difficulty getting certification or licensing later on.

Course work tends to vary from school to school. NGH-certified instructors, however, teach a standard curriculum. Dr. Dwight Damon explains that this way, the association knows its students are getting the same basic education no matter where they're located in the world. "The core curricula is a work in progress; we keep adding to it," says Damon. It is built on what he describes as a "basic, classic approach to hypnosis," including study of and practice in hypnosis techniques, such as progressive relaxation, introduction to psychology, introduction to ethics, and practical information about running your own business. You are not taught how to be a psychologist, psychiatrist, or counselor, Damon emphasizes, but you must be able to refer people to these professionals for serious problems.

If you want to use hypnosis with a medical, dental, psychological, social work, religious, or other profession, you will first need to earn your college and, in some cases, advanced degree in the particular field that interests you and then pursue training in hypnosis. Some medical and dental schools now offer courses in clinical hypnosis, although, again, this is still relatively rare. The major professional associations also provide certification in clinical hypnosis.

Certification or Licensing

A number of associations offer certification, but the two best-known certifying groups are ACHE and NGH. ACHE offers two levels of certification: certified hypnotherapist and certified clinical hypnotherapist. To attain the certified hypnotherapist designation, you must complete at least 200 hours of instruction from an approved school and pass a written and practical skills exam. To attain the certified clinical hypnotherapist designation, you must complete at least 300 hours of instruction from an approved school and pass an examination. The NGH also offers a certification for instructors. Certification is highly recommended because it demonstrates both to your peers and your clients that you have received thorough training and are keeping up with developments in the field.

While most states do not license hypnotherapists, legislation for licensure is being considered in many states. You will need to check with your state's licensing board for specific requirements in your area. In addition, hypnotherapists who run their own businesses will need a business license.

Other Requirements

In order to succeed as a hypnotherapist, you should be able to inspire trust in others. Because you will be asking clients to let their guards down and become open to a higher level of suggestibility, they will need to feel very comfortable with you. A calm, soothing personality, and a voice to match, will help you ease clients into a hypnotic state. You will also need to be able to interact well with a variety of people and have a true interest in helping them. Because hypnotherapy works differently for each person, you should be creative and patient in your approach to your clients and their needs.

Finally, hypnotherapists need high moral and ethical standards. People who seek out hypnotherapy to help overcome a particular obstacle are often very vulnerable, either professionally or personally. A high-profile government leader, for instance, may look to hypnotherapy to help him overcome an addiction to prescription painkillers. Practitioners of hypnotherapy must be sensitive to their clients' needs and wishes and take privacy issues very seriously.

EXPLORING

If you are interested in doing hypnotherapy work, you should contact a professional hypnotherapist organization for guidance. You may qualify for a student membership. Also, many associations hold workshops or have conferences in all areas of the country (and world) throughout the year. Find out how you can attend such a session.

Check out books on hypnotherapy and self-hypnotism from your local library. These guides can teach you the theoretical basis of hypnotism as well as help you learn techniques to apply hypnotism to yourself and your own needs.

Volunteer at a local hospital, hospice, or other extended care facility that employs hypnotherapists as part of their treatment programs. You may be allowed to sit in on a hypnotherapy session or talk to patients to see what progress they make with hypnotism.

Make an appointment to see a hypnotherapist yourself to get a feel for the field. Your hypnotherapist may help you learn more about how you respond to hypnotic suggestion and how you can help others through hypnotherapy.

EMPLOYERS

Because many professionals use hypnosis as part of another career, it's difficult to list all possible places a hypnotherapist may work.

The health fields, of course, are the main arenas for hypnotherapists. A dentist may use hypnosis to help a patient deal with the pain of a root canal, or a psychologist may prescribe hypnotherapy to a client who is having an extended bout of insomnia. Hospitals may have hypnotherapists on call to assist with an emergency room patient, or emergency medical technicians may use hypnosis techniques to help injured people on the scene. A nurse-midwife may use hypnosis to help pregnant women ease the pain of childbirth, or a sports physician may help a football player ease the pain of an injury.

Hypnotherapists work in all fields of medicine: medicine for the body and medicine for the mind. Hypnotherapists work in hospitals, clinics, medical practices, and social and religious organizations. They work as counselors or advisers. A hypnotherapist may work as a teacher of hypnosis or as a consultant.

STARTING OUT

Most people who practice hypnotherapy as their primary occupation set up and run their own businesses. After becoming certified and getting a business license, they rent office space or work out of their homes and start advertising for business. They may network with doctors, dentists, and psychologists to develop a client base. New hypnotherapists may arrange to speak to community, church, or professional groups to educate the public and attract clients. They may also advertise in local newspapers, distribute brochures, or set up a Web site to announce their services. Some hypnotherapists rent space in a medical office suite and build a clientele with the office's patients.

Few professionals rely on hypnotherapy alone; the vast majority of practitioners use hypnotherapy as part of another health-related profession. Therefore, most certified hypnotherapists begin practicing in their primary field first, and then incorporate hypnotherapy into treatments. They may begin by identifying a patient who may be particularly responsive to hypnosis. After suggesting hypnotherapy as a treatment option, the hypnotherapist and the patient work together to deal with the patient's needs through hypnosis. As practitioners become more accomplished using hypnotherapy as part of their practices, they may branch out into using hypnosis for more of their patients, or they may even move toward hypnotherapy as a primary career.

ADVANCEMENT

Hypnotherapists with their own businesses can build on their knowledge and skills. Research in the field continues, and hypnotherapists need to make sure they know all the latest techniques. They can learn and become certified in more counseling or healing arts practices. They can also market their services more aggressively to build a larger client base.

Those in medical or other fields also need to keep their skills up-to-date. They can study hypnosis techniques at the doctoral or postdoctoral level. Practitioners with advanced study and more credentials can usually command higher salaries. Some professional associations now award advanced credentials and recognition to exceptional hypnotherapists. This may include awards for outstanding contributions to the field.

Accomplished hypnotherapists may also move away from client interaction and more toward the administration of hypnotherapy programs. They may focus their time on research in the field, writing books, or publishing papers in professional hypnotherapy or medical research journals. Hypnotherapists may become instructors of hypnosis, or they may use their training and experience to help them pursue an advanced degree in another medical field that may be enriched by hypnotherapy techniques.

EARNINGS

Salaries for people who do hypnosis for a living vary widely. A hypnotherapist in a large urban area may charge from $50 per hour to $150 per hour, depending on his or her experience and ability.

Many people practice hypnotherapy part time while others combine it with another job. According to the Hypnotherapy Academy of America, an ACHE-approved school, a certified hypnotherapist can earn $45,000 or more per year. Average salaries for medical professionals like doctors or dentists may be well over $100,000 per year.

According to the National Board for Professional and Ethical Standards, Hypnosis Education and Certification, a qualified hypnotherapist can earn between $75 and $175 an hour. Many practitioners working part time with four or five clients can earn $400 to $600 a week. Full-time professionals can earn $75,000 or more a year.

Hypnotherapists who work for an established hospital, school, or other company generally enjoy a full complement of benefits, including paid vacation time, sick days, and medical and dental care. Self-employed practitioners must take care of their own benefits.

WORK ENVIRONMENT

People who use hypnotherapy as part of a medical practice generally work in clean, comfortable, soothing surroundings. Because hypnotherapists work to put their patients into a calm, relaxed state for treatment, most offices will be free of extra noise, light, and other distractions. Hypnotherapists often have a monotonous noise-maker—such as a metronome or loud clock—for patients to focus on while they are being hypnotized. The patient may be seated in a comfortable chair or lying down on a sofa.

Practitioners who use hypnotherapy as part of an emergency medical team, such as EMTs, will have a much more frenzied environment. They use hypnotherapy techniques in emergency (and often dangerous) situations, and they need to be prepared for any eventuality.

OUTLOOK

There has been a growing acceptance of hypnotherapy by the conventional medical establishment and the general public over the past decade. According to the *Occupational Outlook Quarterly*, the best opportunities in hypnotherapy are for those who add hypnosis skills to other medical or therapeutic skills, such as dentistry or psychology. People trained only in hypnotherapy generally have a more difficult path. Working for themselves, they need to advertise their services and develop a client base. It can take time to build up a business to the point where it can support you. Competition may also be tough, especially in areas where hypnotism is popular, such as California. Hypnotherapists with limited training often drop out of the field.

In some states, legislation may have an impact on the extent to which hypnotherapy can be practiced and who can practice it.

FOR MORE INFORMATION

Visit this professional organization's Web site to read articles about hypnotherapy.
American Association of Professional Hypnotherapists
4149-A El Camino Way
Palo Alto, CA 94306-4036
Tel: 650-323-3224
http://www.aaph.org

For information on certification and approved programs, contact
American Council of Hypnotist Examiners
700 South Central Avenue
Glendale, CA 91204-2011
Tel: 818-242-1159
Email: hypnotismla@earthlink.net
http://www.hypnotistexaminers.org

For certification and degree programs in hypnotherapy, contact
American Pacific University
615 Piikoi Street, Suite 501
Honolulu, HI 96814-3140
Tel: 800-800-6463
http://www.ampac.edu

The NGH is one of the oldest hypnotherapy organizations in the United States. For information on certification and hypnotherapy, contact
National Guild of Hypnotists (NGH)
PO Box 308
Merrimack, NH 03054-0308
Tel: 603-429-9438
Email: ngh@ngh.net
http://www.ngh.net

Kinesiologists

OVERVIEW

Kinesiologists (also known as *kinesiotherapists*) are health care workers who plan and conduct exercise programs to help their clients develop or maintain endurance, strength, mobility, and coordination. Many of their clients are people who have disabilities. They also work with people who are recovering from injuries or illnesses and need help to keep their muscle tone during long periods of inactivity.

Kinesiology is based on the belief that each muscle in the body relates to a specific meridian—or energy pathway—in the body. These meridians also relate to organs, allowing the muscles to give us information about organ function and energy. The profession builds on basic principles from Chinese medicine, acupressure, and massage therapy to bring the body into balance. The goal is to release physical and mental pain, and alleviate tension in the mind and body. Relieving stress—be it physical, mental, emotional, chemical, environmental, or behavioral—is a main element of kinesiology. Various techniques are combined with visualization, massage, and movement exercises to help patients heal.

HISTORY

Kinesiology studies how the principles of mechanics and anatomy affect human movement. The word *kinesio* is derived from the Greek word *kinesis*, meaning motion. Kinesiology literally means the study of motion, or motion therapy. Kinesiology is based on the idea that physical education is a science.

Scientists throughout the centuries have studied how the body works: how muscles are connected, how bones grow, how blood flows. Kinesiology builds on all that knowledge. The practice of kinesiology developed during World War II, when physicians in military hospitals saw that appropriate exercise could help wounded patients heal faster and with better results than they had before. This exercise therapy proved particularly useful for injuries to the arms and legs.

By 1946, Veterans Administration hospitals were using prescribed exercise programs in rehabilitation treatment. Before long, other hospitals and clinics recognized the benefits of kinesiology and instituted similar programs. Within a few years the new therapy was an important part of many treatment programs, including programs for chronically disabled patients.

In the 1950s, a number of studies indicated that European children were more physically fit than American children. To decrease the gap in fitness levels, the United States government instituted physical fitness programs in schools. This practical application of kinesiology to otherwise healthy children boosted the field dramatically.

Today, the study of physical fitness and the movement of the body are illustrated in countless fields. Although kinesiologists have historically worked with injured or disabled patients, as humans move toward a more computerized, less active lifestyle, kinesiologists and other health care professionals will be in higher demand to help people of all abilities maintain good health and fitness.

THE JOB

Kinesiology is a broad field covering the study of how muscles act and coordinate to move the body. Many diverse career opportunities are open to those who have studied kinesiology; for example, jobs in this area include physical education or dance teachers, coaches of sports teams, health and fitness consultants, athletic or personal trainers, and researchers in biomechanics. Kinesiologists are usually identified by their specialty, such as athletic trainer, but for the purposes of this article we will examine the broader, interchangeable titles of kinesiologist and kinesiotherapist. All kinesiologists use muscle testing and physical therapy to evaluate and correct the state of various bodily functions in their patients. Kinesiologists take all body systems into account when treating a patient. And that is the most important aspect of kinesiology: Its aim is to treat the whole patient, not to correct a disorder. Kinesiologists allow patients to work through a disability or disorder.

Kinesiologists work with a wide range of people, both individually and in groups. Their patients may be disabled children or adults, geriatric patients, psychiatric patients, the developmentally disabled, or amputees. Some may have had heart attacks, strokes, or spinal injuries. Others may be affected by such conditions as arthritis, impaired circulation, or cerebral palsy. Kinesiologists also work with people who were involved in automobile accidents, have congenital birth defects, or have sustained sports injuries.

These professionals work to help their clients be more self-reliant, enjoy leisure activities, and even adapt to new ways of living, working, and thriving. Although kinesiologists work with their patients physically, giving them constant encouragement and emotional support is also an important part of their work.

Kinesiologists' responsibilities may include teaching patients to use artificial limbs or walk with canes, crutches, or braces. They may help visually impaired people learn how to move around without help or teach patients who cannot walk how to drive cars with hand controls. For mentally ill people, therapists may develop therapeutic activities that help them release tension or teach them how to cooperate with others.

The work is often physically demanding. Kinesiologists work with such equipment as weights, pulleys, bikes, and rowing machines. They demonstrate exercises so their patients can learn to do them and also may teach members of their patients' families to help the patients exercise. They may work with their patients in swimming pools, whirlpools, saunas, or other therapeutic settings. When patients are very weak or have limited mobility, therapists may help them exercise by lifting them or moving their limbs.

Kinesiologists work as members of medical teams. Physicians describe the kind of exercise their patients should have, and then the therapists develop programs to meet the specific needs of the patients. Other members of the medical team may include nurses, psychologists, psychiatrists, social workers, massage therapists, physical therapists, acupuncturists, and vocational counselors.

Kinesiologists write reports on the clients' progress to provide necessary information for other members of the medical team. These reports, which describe the treatments and their results, may also provide useful information for researchers and other members of the health care team.

These therapists do not do the same work as physical therapists, orthotists, or prosthetists. *Physical therapists* test and measure the functions of the musculoskeletal, neurological, pulmonary, and cardiovascular systems and treat the problems that occur in these systems. (See the article Physical Therapists.) *Orthotists* are concerned with supporting and bracing weak or ineffective joints and muscles, and *prosthetists* are concerned with replacing missing body parts with artificial devices. Kinesiologists focus instead on the interconnection of all these systems. In certain cases, they may refer a patient to another specialist for additional treatment.

REQUIREMENTS

High School

If you are interested in this field, you should prepare for your college studies by taking a strong college-preparatory course load. Classes in anatomy, chemistry, biology, mathematics, and physics will give you the basic science background you will need to study kinesiology in college. Health, psychology, and social science will also be very helpful. Be sure to take physical education classes in order to gain a better appreciation for the nature of movement and our muscles. Participating in a sport will also help you learn more about kinesiology from an inside perspective.

Postsecondary Training

In order to practice kinesiology, you will need to earn a bachelor's degree from a four-year program at an accredited school. Curriculum standards have been established by the Committee on Accreditation of Education Programs for Kinesiotherapy, which also reviews programs and makes recommendations for accreditation to the Commission on Accreditation of Allied Health Education Programs (CAAHEP). To find out more about accredited programs, visit the CAAHEP's Web site, http://www.caahep.org. Some kinesiologists major in physical education, exercise science, or health science and have kinesiology as a specialty, but a growing number of institutions in the United States are starting to offer undergraduate degrees in kinesiology. Approved programs include classes in education, clinical practice, biological sciences, and behavioral sciences. Specific courses may have titles such as Movement Coordination, Control, and Skill; Performance and Physical Activity; Biomechanics; Developmental Games; Personal and Community Health; and Motor Learning. Master's degrees in kinesiology and related programs are currently offered at more than 100 institutions; doctorates in the field are offered at approximately 55 universities.

Clinical internships are also required. These internships generally consist of at least 1,000 hours of training at an approved health facility under the supervision of certified kinesiologists. You may also seek out an assistantship with a practicing kinesiologist.

Certification or Licensing

Although certification is not mandatory for every job, it is highly recommended as a way of showing professional achievement. Certification is offered in the form of registration by the Council on Professional Standards for Kinesiotherapy (COPS-KT) through the American Kinesiotherapy Association. To receive registration from COPS-KT, applicants must have at least a bachelor's degree in kinesiotherapy, exercise science, or a related field, complete core course requirements as specified by COPS-KT, have at least 1,000 hours of clinical experience under the supervision of a registered kinesiotherapist, and pass an examination. Those who meet these requirements receive the designation registered kinesiotherapist. To keep this designation, kinesiotherapists must complete continuing education credits each year.

If a kinesiotherapist has earned an undergraduate degree in physical education, he or she also may become a state-certified physical education teacher after meeting the certification requirements for his or her state.

Other certifications are available based on the kinesiologist's specialty. For example, the American College of Sports Medicine offers certifications for health and fitness instructors, specialists, and physiologists. Athletic trainers are certified by the Board of Certification for the National Athletic Trainers' Association. Such certifications typically require having completed an accredited education program as well as passing an exam.

Other Requirements

To work as a kinesiologist, you must be mature and objective and able to work well with patients and other staff members. You must have excellent communication skills to explain the exercises so patients can understand your instructions and perform the exercises properly.

You will also need stamina to demonstrate the exercises and help patients with them. You should be patient since many exercise programs are repetitive and are carried out over long periods. A good sense of humor also helps to keep up patient morale. As a kinesiologist, you also must know how to plan and carry out a program, and stay current on new developments in the field. Certification usually requires continuing education courses.

EXPLORING

If you are a high school student interested in this type of work, you can get experience in several ways. Basic physical education courses as well as team sports, like volleyball or track, will help you gain an appreciation for the possibilities and limitations of the body. Plan and carry out exercise programs, or instruct others in proper exercise techniques. Many exercise classes are often offered in scouting and by organizations such as the YMCA and YWCA.

Opportunities for volunteer, part-time, or summer work may be available at facilities that have kinesiology or kinesiotherapy programs, such as hospitals, clinics, nursing homes, and summer camps for disabled children. Health and exercise clubs also may have summer work or part-time jobs. In addition, you may be able to visit kinesiology departments at health care centers to talk with staff members and see how they work.

EMPLOYERS

Kinesiologists work in many types of organizations. They work for the government in the Department of Veterans Affairs, public and private hospitals, sports medicine facilities, and rehabilitation facilities. Learning disability centers, grammar schools and high schools, colleges and universities, and health clubs also employ kinesiologists. Other kinesiologists work in private practice or as exercise consultants. Kinesiologists can also find employment with sports teams, or they may write for or edit sports, rehabilitative, and other medical journals. Many kinesiologists also teach in the field or do research.

STARTING OUT

The American Kinesiotherapy Association maintains an employment service for certified kinesiologists and kinesiotherapists. Plus, most colleges and universities offer job placement assistance for their alumni. Therapists also may apply at health facilities that have kinesiotherapy programs, including private and state hospitals, Department of Veterans Affairs hospitals, clinics, health clubs, chiropractic clinics, and rehabilitation centers. Many kinesiologists find employment by networking with other professionals in the field. Most professional organizations and associations maintain listings of positions open in various locations.

Beginning kinesiologists may gain paid employment with a facility if they start out doing volunteer work. Some organizations prefer to hire therapists with some work experience, and volunteer work gives the new kinesiotherapist a great opportunity to learn more about the field and a particular organization.

ADVANCEMENT

Kinesiologists usually start as staff therapists at hospitals, clinics, or other health care facilities. After several years, they may become supervisors or department heads. Some move on to do consultant work for health care facilities. Some kinesiologists use their practical experience to do more research in the field, or they may teach at a kinesiology program. They may write for field newsletters or journals, reporting on their progress in rehabilitating a particular patient or in treating a specific disability. With advanced training, experienced kinesiologists may go on to more senior positions at health care centers, clinics, colleges, and related facilities.

EARNINGS

According to the American Kinesiotherapy Association, the average starting salary for kinesiologists is between $34,000 and $37,000. This, of course, depends on the experience of the kinesiologist and the location of the job. Since kinesiology is a relatively new field, few reliable salary sources exist, but salaries are probably comparable to related health professions.

According to 2006 information from the U.S. Department of Labor, the median salary for occupational therapy assistants was $42,060, while the median for occupational therapists was $60,470. Kinesiologist salaries are likely to be somewhere in those ranges. Those working in hospitals tended to earn less than those in private practice.

Depending on their employers, most kinesiologists enjoy a full complement of benefits, including vacation and sick time as well as holidays and medical and dental insurance. Kinesiologists who work in a health care facility usually get free use of the exercise equipment.

WORK ENVIRONMENT

Kinesiologists who work in hospitals and clinics usually work a typical 40-hour workweek, with hours somewhere between 8:00 A.M. and 6:00 P.M., Monday through Friday. Some may work evenings and weekends instead in order to accommodate their clients' schedules. Because of the long-range, rehabilitative nature of the work, most kinesiologists work a set schedule and generally don't have to be available for emergency situations.

The number of patients the therapist works with usually depends on the size and function of the facility. When leading a rehabilitation group, the kinesiologist may work with three to five patients at a time, helping them work on their own and as part of a team. Therapists may see their patients in hospitals and other health centers, or they may visit patients in their homes, or arrange for rehabilitative outings. Their clients may be confined to beds, chairs, or wheelchairs. Exercises are often performed in pools or on ramps, stairways, or exercise tables.

OUTLOOK

Employment for kinesiologists is expected to grow about as fast as the average for all occupations for the next few years. The demand for their services may grow somewhat because of the increasing emphasis on services for disabled people, patients with specific disorders, and the growing number of older adults. Some medical workers also handle patients with chronic pain by using the physical rehabilitation and retraining at the base of kinesiology. Plus, kinesiology is certain to grow as a profession as more is learned about the field.

As health costs rise, the importance of outpatient care is expected to increase as well. Many insurance companies prefer to pay for home health care or outpatient care instead of lengthy, expensive—and often unnecessary—hospital stays. Part-time workers in the field will also see increased opportunities. In addition, openings will occur as many of the early kinesiotherapists reach retirement age and others change jobs or leave for other reasons.

FOR MORE INFORMATION

For career information, contact
American Academy of Kinesiology and Physical Education
c/o Human Kinetics
PO Box 5076
Champaign, IL 61820-2200
Tel: 800-747-4457
Email: kims@aakpe.org
http://www.aakpe.org

The AAHPERD is an umbrella organization for a number of groups dedicated to health and fitness. For more detailed information on kinesiology and related fields, contact
American Alliance for Health, Physical Education, Recreation
  and Dance (AAHPERD)
1900 Association Drive
Reston, VA 20191-1598
Tel: 800-213-7193
Email: info@aahperd.org
http://www.aahperd.org

For more information about education and certification, contact
American Kinesiotherapy Association
118 College Drive, #5142
Hattiesburg, MS 39406-0001

Tel: 800-296-2582
Email: info@akta.org
http://www.akta.org

For information on accredited programs, contact
**Commission on Accreditation of Allied Health Education
  Programs**
1361 Park Street
Clearwater, FL 33756-6039
Tel: 727-210-2350
Email: mail@caahep.org
http://www.caahep.org

To learn more about biomechanics, visit this society's Web site.
American Society of Biomechanics
http://www.asbweb.org

For information on kinesiology, contact
International College of Applied Kinesiology
http://www.icak.com

*This University of Illinois at Urbana-Champaign Web site provides
links to many kinesiology-related resources.*
The Kinesiology Forum
http://www.kines.uiuc.edu/kinesforum

INTERVIEW

*Melissa Fuller is the executive director of the American Kinesio-
therapy Association and teaches kinesiotherapy at the University
of Southern Mississippi (Hattiesburg). She has been a registered
kinesiotherapist since July 2001. Melissa discussed the field with
the editors of* Careers in Focus: Therapists.

Q. Why did you decide to enter the field?
A. I have always been interested in the effects diet and exercise
have on health and fitness. The kinesiotherapy curriculum was
a good fit for me because it gave me the professional skills to
help others improve their health through exercise.

**Q. What is one thing that young people may not know about
a career in kinesiotherapy?**
A. A career in kinesiotherapy offers a wide variety of employment
opportunities. With the training and knowledge a kinesiotherapist

possesses they are uniquely qualified to work with medically stable clients with functional disabilities due to the effects of injury, illness, chronic disease, or congenital disorders. Kinesiotherapists also possess the basic knowledge in fitness and exercise to work with the healthy population for improved fitness.

Q. What types of students pursue study in kinesiotherapy in your program?

A. The role of the kinesiotherapist demands intelligence, judgment, honesty, interpersonal skills, and the capacity to react to emergencies in a calm and reasonable manner. An attitude of respect for self and others, adherence to the concepts of privilege and confidentiality in communicating with patients, and a commitment to the patient's welfare are standard attributes. At a minimum, a kinesiotherapist is educated in areas of basic exercise science and clinical applications of rehabilitation exercise. Training is received in orthopedic, neurological, psychiatric, pediatric, cardiovascular-pulmonary, and geriatric practice settings.

Q. Where do kinesiotherapists find employment?

A. Registered kinesiotherapists are employed in Department of Veterans Affairs medical centers, public and private hospitals, medical fitness facilities, rehabilitation facilities, learning disability centers, schools, colleges and universities, private practice, and as exercise consultants.

Q. Tell us about the work of the American Kinesiotherapy Association. How important is membership in professional associations to career success?

A. The mission of the American Kinesiotherapy Association (AKTA) is to promote kinesiotherapy and improve recognition of the profession through the pursuit of legislation and public relations. The AKTA serves the interests of its members and will work to enhance the standard of care provided by kinesiotherapists through educational opportunities. Members of the AKTA receive a tri-annual newsletter, access to the association's Web site, access to the journal *Clinical Kinesiology*, and discounts on yearly conference fees. All of these things help members of the profession keep up-to-date on current events, job announcements, and other news in regards to professional development.

Massage Therapists

OVERVIEW

Massage therapy is a broad term referring to a number of health-related practices, including Swedish massage, sports massage, Rolfing, shiatsu and acupressure, trigger point therapy, and reflexology. Although the techniques vary, most *massage therapists* (or *massotherapists*) press and rub the skin and muscles. Relaxed muscles, improved blood circulation and joint mobility, reduced stress and anxiety, and decreased recovery time for sprains and injured muscles are just a few of the potential benefits of massage therapy. Massage therapists are sometimes called *bodyworkers*. The titles *masseur* and *masseuse,* once common, are now rare among those who use massage for therapy and rehabilitation. There are approximately 97,000 massage therapists employed in the United States.

HISTORY

Getting a massage used to be considered a luxury reserved only for the very wealthy, or an occasional splurge for the less affluent. Some people thought massage to be a cover for illicit activities such as prostitution. With increased regulation of certification and a trend toward ergonomics in the home and workplace, however, massage therapy is recognized as an important tool in both alternative and preventative health care. Regular massage can help alleviate physical ailments faced by people today: physical stress brought on by an increase in sedentary lifestyle, aches and pains from hours spent in front of the computer, as well as injuries of the weekend warrior trying to make up for five days of inactivity.

THE JOB

Massage therapists work to produce physical, mental, and emotional benefits through the manipulation of the body's soft tissue. Auxiliary methods, such as the movement of joints and the application of dry and steam heat, are also used. Among the potential physical benefits are the release of muscle tension and stiffness, reduced blood pressure, better blood circulation, a shorter healing time for sprains and pulled muscles, increased flexibility and greater range of motion in the joints, and reduced swelling from edema (excess fluid buildup in body tissue). Massage may also improve posture, strengthen the immune system, and reduce the formation of scar tissue.

Mental and emotional benefits include a relaxed state of mind, reduced stress and anxiety, clearer thinking, and a general sense of well-being. Physical, mental, and emotional health are all interconnected: Being physically fit and healthy can improve emotional health, just as a positive mental attitude can bolster the immune system to help the body fight off infection. A release of muscle tension also leads to reduced stress and anxiety, and physical manipulation of sore muscles can help speed the healing process.

There are many different approaches a massage therapist may take. Among the most popular are Swedish massage, sports massage, Rolfing, shiatsu and acupressure, and trigger point therapy.

In Swedish massage the traditional techniques are effleurage, petrissage, friction, and tapotement. Effleurage (stroking) uses light and hard rhythmic strokes to relax muscles and improve blood circulation. It is often performed at the beginning and end of a massage session. Petrissage (kneading) is the rhythmic squeezing, pressing, and lifting of a muscle. For friction, the fingers, thumb, or palm or heel of the hand are pressed into the skin with a small circular movement. The massage therapist's fingers are sometimes pressed deeply into a joint. Tapotement (tapping), in which the hands strike the skin in rapid succession, is used to improve blood circulation.

During the session the client, covered with sheets, lies undressed on a padded table. Oil or lotion is used to smooth the skin. Some massage therapists use aromatherapy, adding fragrant essences to the oil to relax the client and stimulate circulation. Swedish massage may employ a number of auxiliary techniques, including the use of rollers, belts, and vibrators; steam and dry heat; ultraviolet and infrared light; and saunas, whirlpools, steam baths, and packs of hot water or ice.

Sports massage is essentially Swedish massage used in the context of athletics. A light massage generally is given before an event or game to loosen and warm the muscles. This reduces the chance of injury and may improve performance. After the event the athlete is massaged more deeply to alleviate pain, reduce stiffness, and promote healing.

Rolfing, developed by American Ida Rolf, involves deep, sometimes painful massage. Intense pressure is applied to various parts of the body. Rolfing practitioners believe that emotional disturbances, physical pain, and other problems can occur when the body is out of alignment—for example, as a result of poor posture. This method takes 10 sessions to complete.

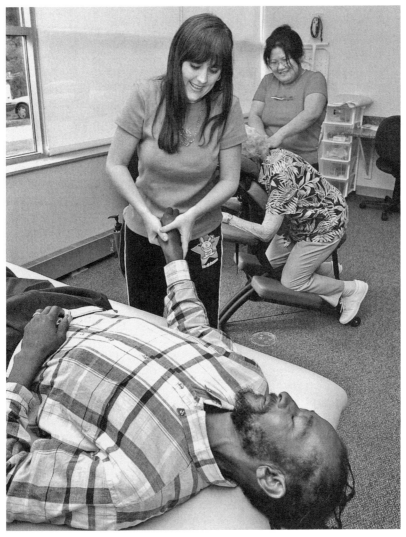

Massage therapists give massages to the elderly at a senior center. *(Johnny Crawford, The Image Works)*

Like the ancient Oriental science of acupuncture, shiatsu and acupressure are based on the concept of meridians, or invisible channels of flowing energy in the body. The massage therapist presses down on particular points along these channels to release blocked energy and untie knots of muscle tension. For this approach the patient wears loosely fitted clothes, lies on the floor or on a futon, and is not given oil or lotion for the skin.

Trigger point therapy, a neuromuscular technique, focuses in on a painful area, or trigger point, in a muscle. A trigger point might be associated with a problem in another part of the body. Using the fingers or an instrument, such as a rounded piece of wood, concentrated pressure is placed on the irritated area in order to "deactivate" the trigger point.

All of these methods of massage can be altered and intermingled depending on the client's needs. Massage therapists can be proficient in one or many of the methods, and usually tailor a session to the individual.

REQUIREMENTS

High School

Since massage therapists need to know more than just technical skills, many practitioners use the basic knowledge learned in high school as a foundation to build a solid career in the field. During your high school years, you should take fundamental science courses, such as chemistry, anatomy, and biology. These classes will give you a basic understanding of the human body and prepare you for the health and anatomy classes you will take while completing your postsecondary education. English, psychology, and other classes relating to communications and human development will also be useful as the successful massage therapist is able to express his or her ideas with clients as well as understand the clients' reactions to the therapy. If you think you might wish to run your own massage therapy business someday, computer and business courses are essential. Finally, do not neglect your own physical well-being. Take physical education and health courses to strengthen your body and your understanding of your own conditioning.

Postsecondary Training

The best way to become a successful massage therapist is to attend an accredited massage therapy school after you have finished high school. There are approximately 300 state-accredited massage schools located throughout the United States. More than 80 of these schools are accredited or approved by the Commission on Massage Therapy Accreditation (COMTA), a major accrediting agency for massage therapy programs and an affiliate of the American Massage Therapy Association (AMTA). COMTA-accredited and -approved schools must provide at least 500 hours of classroom instruction. Studies should include such courses as anatomy, physiology, theory and practice of massage therapy, and ethics. In addition, students should receive supervised hands-on experience. Most programs offer students the opportunity to participate at clinics, such as those providing massage services at hospices, hospitals, and shelters, or at school clinics that are open to the general public.

Massage therapy training programs typically take about a year to complete. Students can specialize in particular disciplines, such as infant massage or rehabilitative massage. Basic first aid and cardiopulmonary resuscitation (CPR) must also be learned. When choosing a school, you should pay close attention to the philosophy and curricula of the program, since a wide range of program options exists. Also, keep in mind that licensure requirements for massage therapists vary by state. For example, some state medical boards require students to have completed more than 500 hours of instruction before they can be recognized as massage therapists. Part of your process for choosing a school, therefore, should include making sure that the school's curriculum will allow you to meet your state's requirements.

Certification or Licensing

Currently, 37 states and the District of Columbia regulate the practice of massage therapy, requiring licensure, certification, or registration. Because requirements for licensing, certification, registration, and even local ordinances vary, however, you will need to check with your state's department of regulatory agencies to get specifics for your area. Typically, requirements include completing an accredited program and passing a written test and a demonstration of massage therapy techniques.

The National Certification Board for Therapeutic Massage and Bodywork offers two national certification examinations for massage therapists: the National Certification Examination for Therapeutic Massage and Bodywork and the National Certification Examination for Therapeutic Massage. To learn more about each exam, visit http://www.ncbtmb.com. Certification is highly recommended, since it demonstrates a therapist's high-level of education and achievement. Certification may also make a therapist a more desirable candidate for job openings.

Employment Settings for Massage Therapists

- Massage offices
- Group practices
- Private practices
- Physicians' offices and clinics
- Chiropractors' offices and clinics
- Community service organizations
- Hospitals and wellness centers
- Nursing homes/hospices
- On-site (chair massage at airports, offices, trade shows, public events, etc.)
- Health clubs and fitness centers
- Sports teams and events (professional and amateur)
- Hotels
- Spas and resorts
- Beauty and hair salons
- Cruise ships
- Country clubs

Source: American Massage Therapy Association

Other Requirements

Physical requirements of massage therapists generally include the ability to use their hands and other tools to rub or press on the client's body. Manual dexterity is usually required to administer the treatments, as is the ability to stand for at least an hour at a time. Special modifications or accommodations can often be made for people with different abilities.

If you are interested in becoming a massage therapist, you should be, above all, nurturing and caring. Constance Bickford, a certified massage therapist in Chicago, thinks that it is necessary to be both flexible and creative: easily adaptable to the needs of the client, as well as able to use different techniques to help the client feel better. Listening well and responding to the client is vital, as is focusing all attention on the task at hand. Massage therapists need to tune in to their client rather than zone out, thinking about the grocery list or what to cook for supper. An effective massage is a mindful one, where massage therapist and client work together toward improved health.

To be a successful massage therapist, you should also be trustworthy and sensitive. Someone receiving a massage may feel awkward lying naked in an office covered by a sheet, listening to music while a stranger kneads his or her muscles. A good massage therapist will make the client feel comfortable in what could potentially be perceived as a vulnerable situation.

Therapists considering opening up their own business should be prepared for busy and slow times. In order to both serve their clients well and stay in business, they should be adequately staffed during rush seasons, and must be financially able to withstand dry spells.

EXPLORING

The best way to become familiar with massage therapy is to get a massage. Look for a certified therapist in your area and make an appointment for a session. If you can afford it, consider going to several different therapists who offer different types of massage. Also, ask if you can set up an informational interview with one of the therapists. Explain that you are interested in pursuing this career and come to the interview prepared to ask questions. What is this massage therapist's educational background? Why was he or she drawn to the job? What is the best part of this work? By talking to a massage therapist, you may also have the chance to develop a mentoring relationship with him or her.

A less costly approach is to find a book on massage instruction at a local public library or bookstore. Massage techniques can then be practiced at home. Books on self-massage are available. Many books discuss in detail the theoretical basis for the techniques. Videos that demonstrate massage techniques are available as well.

Consider volunteering at a hospice, nursing home, or shelter. This work will give you experience in caring for others and help you develop good listening skills. It is important for massage therapists to listen well and respond appropriately to their clients' needs. The massage therapist must make clients feel comfortable, and volunteer work can help foster the skills necessary to achieve this.

EMPLOYERS

Approximately 97,000 massage therapists are employed in the United States. After graduating from an accredited school of massage therapy, there are a number of possibilities for employment. Doctors' offices, hospitals, clinics, health clubs, resorts, country clubs, cruise ships, community service organizations, and nursing homes, for example, all employ massage therapists. Some chiropractors have a massage therapist on staff to whom they can refer patients. A number of massage therapists run their own businesses. Most opportunities for work will be in larger, urban areas with population growth, although massage therapy is slowly spreading to more rural areas as well.

STARTING OUT

There are a number of resources you can use to locate a job. The AMTA offers job placement information to certified massage therapists who belong to the organization. Massage therapy schools have career services offices. Newspapers often list jobs. Some graduates are able to enter the field as self-employed massage therapists, scheduling their own appointments and managing their own offices.

Networking is a valuable tool in maintaining a successful massage therapy enterprise. Many massage therapists get clients through referrals, and often rely on word of mouth to build a solid customer base. Beginning massage therapists might wish to consult businesses about arranging onsite massage sessions for their employees.

Health fairs are also good places to distribute information about massage therapy practices and learn about other services in the industry. Often, organizers of large sporting events will employ massage therapists to give massages to athletes at the finish line. These events may include marathons and runs or bike rides held to raise money for charitable organizations.

ADVANCEMENT

For self-employed massage therapists, advancement is measured by reputation, the ability to attract clients, and the fees charged for services. Health clubs, country clubs, and other institutions have supervisory positions for massage therapists. In a community service organization, massage therapists may be promoted to the position of health service director. Licensed massage therapists often become instructors or advisors at schools for massage therapy. They may also make themselves available to advise individuals or companies on the short- and long-term benefits of massage therapy, and how massage therapy can be introduced into professional work environments.

EARNINGS

The earnings of massage therapists vary greatly with the level of experience and location of practice. Therapists in New York and

California, for example, typically charge higher rates than those in other parts of the country. Some entry-level massage therapists earn as little as minimum wage (ending up with a yearly income of around $12,170), but with experience, a massage therapist can charge from $45 to $70 for a one-hour session.

The U.S. Department of Labor reports that massage therapists earned a median salary of $33,400 a year in 2006. The lowest paid 10 percent earned $15,550 or less, while the highest paid 10 percent earned $70,360 or more.

An article in *USA Today* profiling the career of massage therapist reported hourly earnings ranging from $40 to $110. Those with earnings at the high end typically worked in higher paying geographic areas (such as large cities), had years of experience, and had built up a large clientele. For therapists who worked in spas, salons, resorts, and gyms, *USA Today* noted earnings of $10 to $30 per hour, plus tips (which can add thousands of dollars to annual incomes). For massage therapists working full time, the article estimated yearly earnings of approximately $35,000 to $40,000. Well-established therapists who manage to schedule an average of 20 clients a week for one-hour sessions can earn more than $40,000 annually.

Approximately two-thirds of all massage therapists are self-employed and are not paid for the time spent on bookkeeping, maintaining their offices, waiting for customers to arrive, and looking for new clients. In addition, they must pay a self-employment tax and provide their own benefits. With membership in some national organizations, self-employed massage therapists may be eligible for group life, health, liability, and renter's insurance through the organization's insurance agency.

Massage therapists employed by a health club usually get free or discounted memberships to the club. Those who work for resorts or on cruise ships can get free or discounted travel and accommodations, in addition to full access to facilities when not on duty. Massage therapists employed by a sports team often get to attend the team's sporting events.

WORK ENVIRONMENT

Massage therapists work in clean, comfortable settings. Because a relaxed environment is essential, the massage room may be dim, and soft music, scents, and oils are often used. Since massage therapists may see a number of people per day, it is important to maintain a hygienic working area. This involves changing sheets on the massage table after each client, as well as cleaning and sterilizing any implements used, and washing hands frequently.

Massage therapists employed by businesses may use a portable massage chair—that is, a padded chair that leaves the client in a forward-leaning position ideal for massage of the back and neck. Some massage therapists work out of their homes or travel to the homes of their clients.

The workweek of a massage therapist is typically 35 to 40 hours, which may include evenings and weekends. On average, 20 hours or fewer per week are spent with clients, and the other hours are spent making appointments and taking care of other business-related details.

Since the physical work is sometimes demanding, massage therapists need to take measures to prevent repetitive stress disorders, such as carpal tunnel syndrome. Also, for their own personal safety, massage therapists who work out of their homes or have odd office hours need to be particularly careful about scheduling appointments with unknown clients.

OUTLOOK

The industry predicts a strong employment outlook for massage therapists through the next several years. The growing acceptance of massage therapy as an important health care discipline has led to the creation of additional jobs for massage therapists in many sectors.

One certified massage therapist points to sports massage as one of the fastest growing specialties in the field. The increasing popularity of professional sports has given massage therapists new opportunities to work as key members of a team's staff. Their growing presence in sports has made massage therapy more visible to the public, spreading the awareness of the physical benefits of massage.

Massages aren't just for athletes. According to a survey by the American Massage Therapy Association, 22 percent of Americans surveyed in August 2005 had a massage in the past 12 months. The survey found that people are getting massages not just for medical reasons, but to relax and reduce stress.

There is a growing opportunity for massage therapists in the corporate world. Many employers eager to hold on to good employees offer perks, such as workplace massages. As a result, many massage therapists are working as mobile business consultants.

FOR MORE INFORMATION

For information on careers and education programs, contact
American Massage Therapy Association
500 Davis Street
Evanston, IL 60201-4668

Tel: 877-905-2700
Email: info@amtamassage.org
http://www.amtamassage.org

For information on careers in the field (including the brochure,
Your Massage & Bodywork Career), *state board requirements, and*
training programs, contact
Associated Bodywork and Massage Professionals
1271 Sugarbush Drive
Evergreen, CO 80439-9766
Tel: 800-458-2267
Email: expectmore@abmp.com
http://www.abmp.com
http://www.massagetherapy.com

For information on accreditation and programs, contact
Commission on Massage Therapy Accreditation
1007 Church Street, Suite 302
Evanston, IL 60201-5912
Tel: 847-869-5039
Email: info@comta.org
http://www.comta.org

For information about state certification and education require-
ments, contact
National Certification Board for Therapeutic Massage and
  Bodywork
1901 South Meyers Road, Suite 240
Oakbrook Terrace, IL 60181-5206
Tel: 800-296-0664
Email: info@ncbtmb.com
http://www.ncbtmb.com

Music Therapists

OVERVIEW

Music therapists treat and rehabilitate people with mental, physical, and emotional disabilities. They use the creative process of music in their therapy sessions to determine the underlying causes of problems and to help patients achieve therapeutic goals. The specific objectives of the therapeutic activities vary according to the needs of the patient and the setting of the therapy program. There are approximately 5,000 music therapists employed in the United States.

HISTORY

Creative arts therapy programs are fairly recent additions to the health care field. Although many theories of mental and physical therapy have existed for centuries, it has been only in the last 70 years or so that health care professionals have truly realized the healing powers of music and other forms of artistic self-expression.

According to the American Music Therapy Association (AMTA), the discipline of music therapy began during World War I, when amateur and professional musicians visited veterans' hospitals to play for the thousands of veterans who were being treated for both physical and emotional maladies caused by the war. Health administrators and physicians recognized that the music positively affected their patients, and music therapists were hired to formally work with patients. The field of music therapy advanced further during and after World War II, when the Department of Veterans Affairs (VA) developed and organized various music and other creative arts activities for patients in VA hospitals. These activities had a dramatic effect on the physical and mental well-being of the veterans, and music and other creative arts therapists began to help treat and rehabilitate patients in other health care settings.

As music therapy grew in popularity, it became evident that formal training was needed for music therapists to be most effective. The first music therapy degree program in the world was founded at Michigan State University in 1944. Today, there are more than 70 AMTA-approved music therapy programs in the United States.

In 1998, the AMTA was founded as a result of a merger between the National Association for Music Therapy and the American Association for Music Therapy. Its oversight of educational programs ensures the professional integrity of music therapists working in the field.

THE JOB

Music therapists use musical lessons and activities to improve a patient's self-confidence and self-awareness, to relieve states of depression, and to improve physical dexterity. For example, a music therapist treating a patient with Alzheimer's disease might play songs from the patient's past in order to stimulate long- and short-term memory, soothe feelings of agitation, and increase a sense of reality. A music therapist treating a patient with a physical disability may have the patient play a keyboard or xylophone to improve their dexterity or have them walk to a musical selection to improve their balance and gait. Music therapists also treat people with mental health needs, learning and developmental disabilities, physical disabilities, brain injuries, conditions related to aging, alcohol and drug abuse problems, and acute and chronic pain.

The main goal of a music therapist is to improve the client's physical, mental, and emotional health. Before therapists begin any treatment, they meet with a team of other health care professionals. After determining the strengths, limitations, and interests of their client, they create a program to promote positive change and growth. The music therapist continues to confer with the other health care workers as the program progresses and adjusts the program according to the client's response to the therapy.

Patients undergoing music therapy do not need to have any special musical ability or be open to one particular musical style. Of course, the patient's personal therapy preferences, physical and mental circumstances, and his or her taste in music (such as a fondness for rap, classical, or country music) will all affect how the music therapist treats the patient.

Music therapists work with all age groups: young children, adolescents, adults, and senior citizens. They work in individual, group, or family sessions. The approach of the therapist, however, depends on the specific needs of the client or group.

Some music therapists may also edit or write publications about music or creative arts therapy, teach music therapy education courses at colleges and universities, work as professional musicians, or specialize in other creative arts therapy careers such as art, dance, or drama therapy.

REQUIREMENTS

High School

To become a music therapist, you will need a bachelor's degree, so take a college preparatory curriculum while in high school. You should become as proficient as possible with music, musical instruments, and musical theory. When therapists work with patients, they must be able to concentrate completely on the patient rather than on learning how to use tools or techniques. A good starting point for an aspiring music therapist is to study piano or guitar.

In addition to courses such as drama, music, and English, you should consider taking introductory classes in psychology. Also, communications classes will give you an understanding of the various ways people communicate, both verbally and nonverbally.

Postsecondary Training

To become a music therapist you must earn at least a bachelor's degree in music therapy. There are more than 70 AMTA-approved college and university music therapy programs in the United States. Typical courses in a bachelor's degree program in music therapy include professional music therapy, music therapy theory, assessment, evaluation, populations served, ethics, and research and clinical interventions. Undergraduates will also take supporting courses in music, psychology, and human physiology.

In most cases, however, you will also need a graduate degree to advance in the field. Graduate school admissions requirements vary by program, so you would be wise to contact the graduate programs you are interested in to find out about their admissions policies. The AMTA provides a list of schools that meet its quality standards at its Web site, http://www.musictherapy.org/handbook/schools.html.

In graduate school, your study of psychology and music will be in-depth. Classes for someone seeking a master's degree in music therapy may include group psychotherapy, foundation of creativity theory, assessment and treatment planning, and music therapy presentation. In addition to classroom study, you will complete an internship or supervised practicum (that is, work with clients). Depending on your program, you may also need to write a thesis or present a final artistic project before receiving your degree.

Certification or Licensing

Students who receive a bachelor's degree in music therapy are eligible to sit for a certification examination offered by the Certification Board for Music Therapists. Therapists who successfully complete this examination may use the designation, board certified music therapist. Music therapists are required to renew this certification every five years by completing continuing education credits or by retaking the certification exam.

Many music therapists hold additional licenses in other fields, such as social work, education, mental health, or marriage and family therapy. In some states, music therapists need to be licensed depending on their place of work. For specific information on licensing, you will need to check with your state's licensing board. Music therapists are also often members of other professional associations, including the American Psychological Association, the American Association for Marriage and Family Therapy, and the American Counseling Association.

Other Requirements

To succeed as a music therapist, you should have a background in and a love of music. You should also have a strong desire to help others seek positive change in their lives. You must be able to work well with other people—both patients and other health professionals—in the development and implementation of therapy programs. You must have the patience and the stamina to teach and practice therapy with patients for whom progress is often very slow because of their various physical and emotional disorders. A therapist must always keep in mind that even a tiny amount of progress might be extremely significant for some patients and their families. A good sense of humor is also a valuable trait.

EXPLORING

To learn more about careers in music therapy, visit the Web site of the AMTA. Talk with people working in the music therapy field and try to arrange to observe a music therapy session. Look for part-time or summer jobs, or volunteer at a hospital, clinic, nursing home, or any of a number of health care facilities. You might also consider becoming a student member of the AMTA. As a membership benefit, you will receive association publications such as the *Journal of Music Therapy* and *Music Therapy Perspectives*.

A summer job as an aide at a camp for children with disabilities, for example, may help provide insight into the nature of music therapy, including both its rewards and its demands. Such experience can be very valuable in deciding if you are suited to handle the inherent frustrations of a therapy career.

EMPLOYERS

Approximately 5,000 music therapists are employed in the United States. They usually work as members of an interdisciplinary health care team that may include physicians, nurses, social workers, psychiatrists, and psychologists. Although often employed in medical and psychiatric hospitals, therapists also work in rehabilitation centers, nursing homes, day treatment facilities, shelters for battered women, pain and stress management clinics, children's homes, substance abuse programs, hospices, and correctional facilities. Others maintain their own private practices. Some music therapists work with children in grammar and high schools, either as therapists or as music teachers. Others teach or conduct research in the creative arts at colleges and universities.

STARTING OUT

Unpaid training internships (see the AMTA's Web site for a list of internship opportunities) or assistantships that students complete during study for a bachelor's degree in music therapy often can lead to a first job in the field. Graduates can use the career services offices at their colleges or universities to help them find positions in the field. AMTA members can also access a list of job openings at the association's Web site.

Music therapists who are new to the field might consider doing volunteer work at a nonprofit community organization, correctional facility, or neighborhood association to gain some practical experience. Therapists who want to start their own practice can host group therapy sessions in their homes. Music therapists may also wish to associate with other members of the alternative health care field in order to gain experience and build a client base.

ADVANCEMENT

With experience, music therapists can move into supervisory, administrative, and teaching positions. Often, the supervision of interns can resemble a therapy session. The interns will discuss their feelings and ask questions they may have regarding their work with clients. How did they handle their clients? What were the reactions to what their clients said or did? What could they be doing to help more? The supervising therapist helps the interns become competent music therapists.

EARNINGS

Salaries for music therapists vary based on experience, level of training and education, and geographic region of practice. Music therapists earned an average annual salary of $43,869 in 2005, according to the *AMTA Member Sourcebook*. Reported annual salaries ranged from $23,000 to $135,000.

According to MENC: The National Association for Music Education, music therapists earn the following annual salaries based on employment setting: hospital-psychiatric facility, $20,000 to $62,000; special education facility, $22,000 to $42,000; clinic for children with disabilities, $15,000 to $70,000; mental health center, $21,000 to $65,000; nursing home, $17,000 to $65,000; correctional facility, $23,000 to $58,000; and private practice, $18,000 to $77,000.

Music therapists in private practice must provide their own benefits, including health insurance.

WORK ENVIRONMENT

Music therapists work a typical 40-hour, five-day workweek; at times, however, they may have to work extra hours. The number of patients under a therapist's care depends on their specific employment setting. Although many therapists work in hospitals, they may also be employed in such facilities as clinics, rehabilitation centers, children's homes, schools, and nursing homes. Some therapists maintain service contracts with several facilities. For instance, a therapist might work two days a week at a hospital, one day at a nursing home, and the rest of the week at a rehabilitation center. This type of work arrangement entails frequent travel from location to location to see patients.

Most buildings are pleasant, comfortable, and clean places in which to work. Experienced music therapists might choose to be self-employed, working with patients in their own studios. In such a case, the therapist might work more irregular hours to accommodate patient schedules. Other therapists might maintain a combination of service contract work with one or more facilities in addition to a private caseload of clients referred to them by other health care professionals. Whether therapists work on service contracts with various facilities or maintain private practices, they must handle all of the business and administrative details and worries that go along with being self-employed.

OUTLOOK

The AMTA predicts a promising future for the field of music therapy. Demand for music therapists will increase as medical professionals and the general public become aware of the benefits gained through music therapy. Although enrollment in college therapy programs is increasing, new graduates are usually able to find jobs. In cases where an individual is unable to find a full-time position, a therapist might obtain service contracts for part-time work at several facilities.

Job openings in facilities such as nursing homes should continue to increase as the elderly population grows over the next few decades. Advances in medical technology and the recent practice of early discharge from hospitals should also create new opportunities in managed care facilities, chronic pain clinics, cancer care facilities, and hospices. The demand for music therapists should continue to increase as more people become aware of the need to help disabled and ill patients in creative ways.

FOR MORE INFORMATION

For comprehensive information about the career of music therapist and a list of approved educational programs, contact
American Music Therapy Association
8455 Colesville Road, Suite 1000
Silver Spring, MD 20910
Tel: 301-589-3300
Email: info@musictherapy.org
http://www.musictherapy.org

For information on certification, contact
Certification Board for Music Therapists
506 East Lancaster Avenue, Suite 102
Downingtown, PA 19335-2776
Tel: 800-765-2268
Email: info@cbmt.org
http://www.cbmt.org

For information on music therapy at the international level, visit the following Web site:
World Federation for Music Therapy
http://www.musictherapyworld.net

Myotherapists

OVERVIEW

Myotherapy is a method of relieving muscle pain and spasms and improving overall circulation through applied pressure to trigger points. Pressure is applied using fingers, knuckles, and elbows. Those who practice myotherapy are called *myotherapists*.

HISTORY

Bonnie Prudden, a fitness and exercise enthusiast, first developed myotherapy in 1976. During the 1970s, Prudden worked for Dr. Janet Travell, the former personal physician to President Kennedy. Together they treated chronic pain using trigger point injection therapy. Prudden would identify the trigger points on the patient's body with ink, then Dr. Travell would inject the sites with a solution of procaine (a type of local anesthetic) and saline. Afterward, Prudden would conduct muscle exercises and teach patients stretching exercises to do at home in order to keep the muscle strong and relaxed. By chance, while working on a patient, Prudden found that by holding the pressure to trigger points for a longer period of time, the same relief was achieved without the use of invasive needles and solutions. By 1979, the Bonnie Prudden School of Physical Fitness and Myotherapy was established in Tucson, Arizona.

THE JOB

Myotherapy, also called trigger point therapy or neuromuscular massage therapy, is a method of relieving pain, improving circulation, and alleviating muscle spasms. Myotherapists identify the source of pain, called a trigger point, and erase it by the use of applied pressure to these tender spots.

Through the Bonnie Prudden School of Physical Fitness and Myotherapy, students are taught the Prudden method of myotherapy, in addition to anatomy, physiology, exercise, and physical fitness. Classes such as modern dance, drawing, and live sculpture are also offered to encourage students to analyze how the human body moves. After completion of the program, students are given an exam and are required to undergo recertification at the school every two years. (See the Certification or Licensing section for more information.)

A first-time consultation begins with a thorough history of the patient. "Many times pain is the result of an old injury or accident," says Janice Stroughton, a certified myotherapist. "It could also occur as the result of the patient's background and lifestyle." Stroughton explains that weakness and muscle injury is accumulated throughout a lifetime. The average age of patients is between 35 and 55 years— "about the time a person's bucket of accumulated trigger points starts to overflow." Once weak spots are created in the muscle, both physical and emotional stress can cause the spots to go into painful spasms. Myotherapists get rid of spasms by using their fingers, knuckles, or elbows to apply pressure to these trigger points. As muscles relax, the patient is relieved of pain. Afterward the muscle is taught to remain loose and lengthened through the use of exercises. Myotherapists also teach the patient several corrective exercises to do at home.

Myotherapy works on pain as long as the source is muscular, not systemic. It has been shown to be effective for alleviating pain caused by arthritis, bursitis, scoliosis, sciatica, and even pain associated with lupus, AIDS, and muscular dystrophy.

Stroughton collected her own trigger points from years of playing tennis. Complications from scoliosis gave her more pain than she could endure. "I first learned about myotherapy from a tennis instructor who had undergone treatments and persuaded me to give the method a try." Stroughton was so convinced of the benefits of myotherapy that she became a myotherapist. Today, Stroughton is a certified myotherapist at the Myotherapy Pain Control Center in Maryland.

Patients are referred to the Pain Control Center by a medical physician, osteopath, chiropractor, or acupuncturist. Usually, patients have already undergone the battery of X rays, tests, and procedures to ensure pain is not structural in origin. For new patients, history and assessment is taken. "Many times chronic pain is caused by occupation, disease, past accident, surgeries, or participation in sports," says Stroughton. Patients then take the Kraus-Weber Minimum Muscular Fitness Test for Key Posture Muscles. Divided into six tests for different muscle masses, it gauges the flexibility and strength of a person's muscles.

Myotherapists use a trigger point pain chart to mark down the sources of a patient's pain. Once a trigger point is found, the patient identifies its intensity by grading it on a scale of one to 10—one being mild, and 10 almost unbearable. Each location is color marked on the paper chart to indicate the type of pain and the date it is erased.

Patients arrive for treatments barefooted and wearing loose clothing. "Patients are encouraged to bring a friend or family member to observe how treatments and exercises are done," explains Stroughton. "That way, the exercises may be repeated correctly at home. Treatments are 50 percent myotherapy and 50 percent corrective exercises." Using the completed pain chart, trigger points are identified and erased. The location of a trigger point determines the amount and length of pressure applied—on the average seven seconds for most body areas and four to five seconds for the face and head. Tools such as the crook (a metal rod shaped like a shepherd's hook) and the bodo (a wooden dowel) are used to give the myotherapist greater extension and also to help fight fatigue. Small bodos are used to work the hands and feet, while larger bodos are helpful in working larger muscle masses such as the quadriceps and gluteus.

Once the muscles are relaxed, they need to be maintained with exercises specially designed for the patient's problem areas. Patients and their helpers are instructed in the proper way to conduct maintenance exercises to help keep the muscles strong and flexible. These exercises also help improve coordination, strength, and posture.

Stroughton's work schedule varies. Phone consultations with patients take up a large part of the day, as does paperwork. She limits herself to two or three patient treatments a day. Myotherapy is physically taxing on the practitioner. "You always risk injuring yourself," says Stroughton. "You need to be aware of how you use your own body."

REQUIREMENTS

High School

Enid Whittaker, a certified myotherapist and instructor, suggests taking anatomy and physiology classes if you are interested in a career in myotherapy. This will help you understand how the human body works. Also, creative classes such as drawing and sculpture, especially of the human body, will foster good hand coordination skills. Physical fitness classes and dance classes are helpful in developing a strong and flexible body. This is important because myotherapy is physically demanding on the therapist. If you are interested in setting up a private practice, Whittaker also suggests taking business classes, such as marketing, accounting, bookkeeping, and computer science.

Certification or Licensing

There are other schools offering classes in myotherapy, but the Bonnie Prudden Myotherapy School is considered the most reputable program available. The school offers a nine-and-a-half month certification program for its graduates. A total of 1,300 hours of program work is completed at the school after which you may sit for the board exam. For recertification every two years, you are required to take continuing education classes (about 45 hours total) covering new techniques.

Certification is also available from other massage therapy schools, usually requiring completion of a series of workshops or seminars. In some states, you must also become a licensed massage therapist before practicing myotherapy.

Other Requirements

"Working with people in pain can sometimes be unpleasant," says Janice Stroughton. "Don't expect cheery faces and pleasant conversation." Patients, many of whom have been suffering with pain for some time, will be grouchy and in a foul mood. Sometimes a good sense of humor is enough to erase a patient's crankiness. Despite having to deal with bad tempers, Stroughton finds reward in helping patients with their problems and offering them relief from pain. "The best part of my job is knowing I made a difference in someone's life, in regards to pain. It is like giving someone new hope." Stroughton quotes her mentor, Bonnie Prudden, when she says, "Pain, not death, is the enemy."

Questions arise during treatment, such as, Should pressure be kept a few seconds longer? Is the patient ready to end his or her sessions? Are these exercises challenging enough? Good intuition is another important quality you will need in order to answer such questions on the spot. While you will learn the basics of myotherapy in school, you'll need instincts and intuition to help you in actual practice.

Because of the repetitive movements used in myotherapy, many practitioners often run the risk of self-injury. It's important to be aware of your body's limitation and not overuse your own muscles and joints. Sometimes, myotherapists need treatment for their own repetitive stress problems.

EXPLORING

If you can afford it, consider going to several different massage therapists who offer different types of massage. Ask if you can set up an informational interview with various kinds of massage therapists, including myotherapists. Explain that you are interested in pursuing this career and come to the interview prepared to ask questions. What is your educational background? Why were you drawn to the job? What is the best part of this work?

A less costly approach is to find books on massage instruction at a local public library or bookstore. Massage techniques can then be practiced at home. Books on self-massage are available. Many books discuss in detail the theoretical basis for the techniques. Videos that demonstrate massage techniques are available as well.

Consider volunteering at a hospice, nursing home, or shelter. This work will give you experience in caring for others and help you develop good listening skills. As a myotherapist, it is important for you to listen well and respond appropriately to your clients' needs. The therapist must make clients feel comfortable, and volunteer work can help you learn the skills necessary to achieve this.

EMPLOYERS

Myotherapists are employed in a number of health care settings. They may work at a physician's clinic, especially one that treats patients with nerve damage or arthritic pain. Others choose to open up their own practice. Remember, though, that in addition to giving treatments, self-employed myotherapists are also responsible for all duties associated with running a business, handling tax concerns, organizing the office space and supplies, and hiring support staff. The reward is having the freedom to determine their own workdays and hours.

Myotherapists can also join an established clinic. Because of the growing interest and acceptance in myotherapy, many clinics have found it necessary to hire more therapists.

Another option is to combine myotherapy training with other disciplines, such as acupuncture, chiropractic, or massage therapy. These therapists can work for massage clinics, day spas, and alternative medicine practices.

STARTING OUT

It may be difficult for new myotherapists to immediately set up their own businesses. Consider applying to clinics or physicians' group practices to see if they might be interested in offering myotherapy as part of their services. Your chances of finding opportunities are better at organizations that concentrate on alternative and integrative medicine. Working in an established clinic or practice will give you experience, help you build a clientele, and generate publicity for your services.

ADVANCEMENT

Career advancement depends on how myotherapists choose to practice. If they opt to open a private practice, then the obvious advancements would be a larger office, a bigger client base, and perhaps having a staff of myotherapists working for them. Those who choose to join an existing practice advance by growing their client base, gaining seniority, or perhaps establishing their own pain clinic. Myotherapists who join a medical practice advance in the form of more responsibilities, a larger salary, or better benefits. Experienced myotherapists may go on to become instructors in massage therapy schools.

EARNINGS

Salaries for this occupation vary depending on the work setting. Enid Whittaker sees four to seven patients per day. The average patient, depending on the type of pain, needs about four to eight visits, with each treatment costing an average of $75. On the high end, a patient may spend up to $600 to finish pain treatment. Of course, some myotherapists opt to schedule more patients daily and may work with different treatment fees. Because of the physical demands of the job, myotherapists often work less than 40 hours a week. A large percentage of practitioners practice part time, from 10 to 20 hours a week.

According to Salary.com, massage therapists' hourly earnings ranged from $50 to over $100. Well-established therapists who manage to schedule an average of 20 clients a week for one-hour sessions can earn more than $40,000 annually. The U.S. Department of Labor reports that the median annual salary for massage therapists was $33,400 in 2006, and salaries ranged from less than $15,550 to $70,360 or more annually.

Myotherapists in private practice must also be responsible for overhead costs, in addition to acquiring health insurance and other benefits. A myotherapist employed full time at a hospital or other clinical setting may enjoy benefits such as health insurance and paid vacation and sick time. Though employed myotherapists may have greater job security and better benefits, they do not have the option of setting their own work schedules and hours that independent myotherapists enjoy.

Enid Whittaker sums it up best when she stresses, "One becomes a myotherapist because of a desire to help others, not to get rich."

WORK ENVIRONMENT

Massage therapists, including myotherapists, work in clean, comfortable settings. It is important to maintain a hygienic working area. This involves changing sheets on the massage table after each client, as well as cleaning and sterilizing any implements used, and washing hands frequently. Myotherapists use massage tables and a variety of tools to manipulate muscles. Their offices have adequate space for teaching exercises and simple exercise equipment.

Since the physical work is sometimes demanding, myotherapists need to take measures to prevent repetitive stress disorders, such as carpal tunnel syndrome. The workweek of a myotherapist is typically 35 to 40 hours, which may include evenings and weekends to accommodate working clients.

OUTLOOK

Even though there are no official figures, the field of myotherapy has grown. The public, especially in the past few decades, has become more proactive when it comes to their bodies and health. Many people are tired of the dependence on traditional medicine and are looking for alternative methods of pain relief. There is a growing acceptance of myotherapy from the public and the medical field. Many physicians, especially those specializing in neurology and rheumatology, are referring patients for myotherapy treatments more and more. Insurance companies, though slowly, are beginning to cover myotherapy treatments.

About 85 percent of the population experiences some sort of pain, most commonly back pain and headaches. Many people's work involves developed movements that are highly repetitive, with little flexibility. A fairly sedentary occupation such as computer programming will usually result in trigger points to the upper and lower back. Construction work, a highly strenuous occupation, will gather trigger points in the back and torso. Chronic pain can also be sports-related. Beside traditional activities like tennis and golf, some people are fascinated with extreme sports such as mountain and rock climbing and snowboarding. Many athletes turn to the benefits of myotherapy as a form of injury prevention and maintenance.

FOR MORE INFORMATION

For more information on myotherapy, contact
Bonnie Prudden Myotherapy
PO Box 65240
Tucson, AZ 85728-5240
Tel: 800-221-4634
Email: info@bonnieprudden.com
http://www.bonnieprudden.com

For information and a directory of certified myotherapists, visit the following Web site:
International Myotherapy Association
Email: info@myotherapy.org
http://www.myotherapy.org

Occupational Therapists

OVERVIEW

Occupational therapists (OTs) select and direct therapeutic activities designed to develop or restore maximum function to individuals with disabilities. There are approximately 92,000 occupational therapists employed in the United States.

HISTORY

Since about the 14th century, physicians have recognized the therapeutic value of providing activities and occupations for their patients. Observations that mental patients tended to recover more quickly from their illnesses if provided with tasks and duties led physicians to involve their patients in such activities as agriculture, weaving, working with animals, and sewing. Over time, this practice became quite common, and the conditions of many patients improved.

Occupational therapy as we know it today had its beginning after World War I. The need to help disabled veterans of that war, and years later the veterans of World War II, stimulated the growth of this field. Even though its inception was in the psychiatric field, occupational therapy has developed an equally important role in other medical fields, including rehabilitation of physically disabled patients.

Traditionally, occupational therapists taught creative arts such as weaving, clay modeling, leatherwork, jewelry making, and other crafts to promote their patients' functional skills. Today, occupational therapists focus more on providing activities that are designed

QUICK FACTS

School Subjects
Biology
Health

Personal Skills
Helping/teaching
Mechanical/manipulative

Work Environment
Primarily indoors
Primarily one location

Minimum Education Level
Bachelor's degree

Salary Range
$40,840 to $60,470 to
$89,450+

Certification or Licensing
Required

Outlook
Much faster than the average

DOT
076

GOE
14.06.01

NOC
3143

O*NET-SOC
29-1122.00

to promote skills needed in daily living, including self-care; employment education and job skills, such as typing, the operation of computers and computer programs, or the use of power tools; and community and social skills.

It is important to note the difference between occupational therapists and physical therapists. Physical therapy is chiefly concerned with helping people with physical disabilities or injuries to regain functions, or adapt to or overcome their physical limitations. Occupational therapists work with physical factors but also the psychological and social elements of their clients' disabilities, helping them become as independent as possible in the home, school, and workplace. Occupational therapists work not only with the physically challenged, but with people who have mental and emotional disabilities as well.

THE JOB

Occupational therapists use a wide variety of activities to help clients attain their goals for productive, independent living. These goals include developing maximum self-sufficiency in activities of daily living, such as eating, dressing, writing, using a telephone and other communication resources, as well as functioning in the community and the workplace.

In developing a therapeutic program for a client, the occupational therapist often works as a member of a team that can include physicians, nurses, psychiatrists, physical therapists, speech therapists, rehabilitation counselors, social workers, and other specialists. OTs use creative, educational, and recreational activities, as well as human ingenuity, in helping people achieve their full potential, regardless of their disabilities. Each therapy program is designed specifically for the individual client.

Occupational therapists help clients explore their likes and dislikes, their abilities, and their creative, educational, and recreational experiences. Therapists help people choose activities that have the most appeal and value for them. For example, an activity may be designed to promote greater dexterity for someone with arthritic fingers. Learning to use an adapted computer might help a young person with a spinal cord injury to succeed in school and career goals. The therapist works with the clients' interests and helps them develop practical skills and functional independence.

The occupational therapist may work with a wide range of clients. They may assist a client in learning to use an artificial limb. Another client may have suffered a stroke or other neurological disability, and the therapist works with the client to redevelop the client's motor functions or re-educate his or her muscle function. Therapists may assist in the growth and development of premature infants, or they may work with disabled children, helping them learn motor skills or develop skills and tools that will aid them in their education and social interaction.

Some therapists also conduct research to develop new types of therapies and activities and to measure the effectiveness of a therapy program. They may also design and make special equipment or splints to help clients perform their activities.

Other duties may include supervision of volunteer workers, student therapists, and occupational therapy assistants who give instruction in a particular skill. Therapists must prepare reports to keep members of the professional team informed.

Chief occupational therapists in a hospital may teach medical and nursing students the principles of occupational therapy. Many occupational therapists have administrative duties such as directing different kinds of occupational therapy programs, coordinating patient activities, and acting as consultants or advisors to local and state health departments, mental health authorities, and the division of vocational rehabilitation.

REQUIREMENTS

High School

Since you will need to get a college degree, taking college preparatory classes in high school is a must. Courses such as biology, chemistry, and health will expose you to the science fields. Other courses, such as art and social sciences, will help give you an understanding of other aspects of your future work. Also important is a strong background in English. Remember, occupational therapy is a career oriented toward helping people. To be able to work with many different people with different needs, you will need excellent communication skills. Also keep in mind that college admission officers will look favorably at any experience you have had working in the health care field, either in volunteer or paid positions.

Postsecondary Training

The American Occupational Therapy Association (AOTA) recommends that students interested in pursuing graduate study in occupational therapy first earn a bachelor's degree in biology, kinesiology, psychology, sociology, anthropology, liberal arts, or anatomy. As an undergraduate, you should take courses that emphasize

An occupational therapist helps an elderly woman improve her balance through walking exercises. *(John Birdsall, The Image Works)*

the biological and behavioral sciences. Your studies should include classes on anatomy, physiology, neurology, psychology, human growth and development, and sociology.

Anyone wishing to receive the professional credential, registered occupational therapist (OTR), from the National Board for Certification in Occupational Therapy (NBCOT) must have completed at least a master's degree in the field. Graduate programs are accredited by the Accreditation Council for Occupational Therapy Education, which is a part of the AOTA. Visit http://www.aota.org/Students/Schools.aspx for a list of accredited programs.

Graduate occupational therapy programs cover general medical and surgical conditions and interpretation of the principles and practice of occupational therapy in pediatrics, psychiatry, orthopedics, general medicine, and surgery. In addition, emphasis is put on research and critical thinking. Management and administration are also covered in graduate programs.

In addition to classroom work, you must complete fieldwork requirements. According to the AOTA, students need to complete the equivalent of 24 weeks of supervised experience working with clients. This may be done on a full-time basis or a part-time (but not less than half-time) schedule. This training must be completed in order to qualify for professional certification.

In addition to these full-time study options, there are a limited number of part-time and evening programs that allow prospective occupational therapists to work in another field while completing their requirements in occupational therapy.

Certification or Licensing

All states and the District of Columbia regulate the practice of occupational therapy through certification and licensing. National certification is granted by the NBCOT. In order to take the NBCOT exam, you must graduate from an accredited program and complete the clinical practice period. Those who pass this written test are given the designation, occupational therapist, registered, and may use the initials OTR after their names. Initial certification is good for five years and must be renewed every five years after that. Many hospitals and other employers require that their occupational therapists have the OTR designation. In addition, the NBCOT offers several specialty certifications, such as board certified in pediatrics. To receive a specialty certification, you must fulfill education and experience requirements as well as pass an exam.

License requirements generally include graduation from an accredited program, passing the NBCOT certification exam, payment of license fees, and, in some cases, passing an exam covering state statutes and regulations. License renewal requirements vary by state.

Other Requirements

In order to succeed as an occupational therapist, you should enjoy working with people. You should have a patient, calm, and compassionate temperament and have the ability to encourage and inspire your clients. Like your clients, you may encounter frustrating situations as a therapist. For example, it can be difficult and stressful when a client does not respond to treatment as you had hoped. In such situations, occupational therapists need to be persistent, not giving up on the client. Imagination and creativity are also important at such times, because you may need to think of new ways to address the client's problem and create new methods or tools for the client to use.

EXPLORING

While in high school, you should meet with occupational therapists, visit the facilities where they work, and gain an understanding of the types of equipment and skills they use. Many hospitals and occupational therapy facilities and departments also have volunteer opportunities, which will give you strong insight into this career.

EMPLOYERS

There are approximately 92,000 occupational therapists at work in hospitals, schools, nursing homes, home health agencies, mental health centers, adult day care programs, outpatient clinics, and residential care facilities. The profession has seen a growing number of therapists becoming self-employed, in either solo or group practice or in consulting firms.

STARTING OUT

Your school's career services office is usually the best place to start your job search as a newly graduated occupational therapist. You may also apply directly to government agencies (such as the U.S. Public Health Service), private hospitals, and clinics. In addition, the AOTA can provide job seekers with assistance through its employment bulletins.

ADVANCEMENT

Newly graduated occupational therapists usually begin as staff therapists and may qualify as senior therapists after several years on the job. The U.S. Army, Navy, Air Force, and the U.S. Public Health Service commission occupational therapists; other branches of the federal service give civil service ratings. Experienced therapists may become directors of occupational therapy programs in large hospitals, clinics, or workshops, or they may become teachers. Some positions are available as program coordinators and as consultants with large institutions and agencies.

A few colleges and health agencies offer advanced courses in the treatment of special disabilities, such as those resulting from cerebral palsy. Some institutions provide in-service programs for therapists.

EARNINGS

According to the U.S. Department of Labor, median salaries for occupational therapists were $60,470 in 2006. The lowest paid 10 percent earned $40,840 or less a year in 2006, and the top 10 percent earned more than $89,450. The AOTA reports that its members earned median annual salaries of $55,800 in 2006.

Salaries for occupational therapists often vary according to where they work. In areas where the cost of living is higher, occupational therapists generally receive higher pay. Occupational therapists employed in public schools earn salaries that vary by school district. In some states, they are classified as teachers and are paid accordingly.

Therapists employed at hospitals and government and public agencies generally receive full benefit packages that include vacation and sick pay, health insurance, and retirement benefits. Self-employed therapists and those who run their own businesses must provide their own benefits.

WORK ENVIRONMENT

Occupational therapists work in occupational therapy workshops or clinics. As mentioned earlier, these workshops or clinics can be found at a variety of locations, such as hospitals, long-term care facilities, schools, and adult day care centers. No matter what the location, though, these workshops and clinics are well-lighted, pleasant settings. Generally, therapists work eight-hour days and 40-hour weeks, with some evening work required in a few organizations.

OUTLOOK

Opportunities for occupational therapists are expected to be highly favorable through 2014 and will grow much faster than the average for all other careers, according to the *Occupational Outlook Handbook*. This growth will occur as a result of the increasing number of middle-aged and elderly people that require therapeutic services. The demand for occupational therapists is also increasing because of growing public interest in and government support for people with disabilities and for occupational therapy programs helping people attain the fullest possible functional status. The demand for rehabilitative and long-term care services is expected to grow strongly over the next decade. There will be numerous opportunities for work with mental health clients, children, and the elderly, as well as with those with disabling conditions.

As the health care industry continues to be restructured, there should be many more opportunities for occupational therapists in nontraditional settings. This factor and proposed changes in the laws should create an excellent climate for therapists wishing to enter private practice. Home health care may experience the greatest growth in the next decade.

FOR MORE INFORMATION

Visit the AOTA's Web site to find out about accredited occupational therapy programs, career information, and news related to the field.
American Occupational Therapy Association (AOTA)
4720 Montgomery Lane
PO Box 31220
Bethesda, MD 20824-1220
Tel: 301-652-2682
http://www.aota.org

For information on certification requirements, contact
National Board for Certification in Occupational Therapy
Eugene B. Casey Building
800 South Frederick Avenue, Suite 200
Gaithersburg, MD 20877-4150
Tel: 301-990-7979
http://www.nbcot.org

Occupational Therapy Assistants and Aides

OVERVIEW

Occupational therapy assistants (also called OTAs) help people with mental, physical, developmental, or emotional limitations using a variety of activities to improve basic motor functions and reasoning abilities. They work under the direct supervision of an occupational therapist, and their duties include helping to plan, implement, and evaluate rehabilitation programs designed to regain patients' self-sufficiency and to restore their physical and mental functions. There are 21,000 occupational therapy assistants employed in the United States. *Occupational therapy aides* help OTAs and occupational therapists by doing such things as clerical work, preparing therapy equipment for a client's use, and keeping track of supplies. Approximately 5,400 occupational therapy aides are employed in the United States.

HISTORY

Since about the 14th century, physicians have recognized the therapeutic value of providing activities and occupations for their patients. Observations that mental patients tended to recover more quickly from their illnesses if provided with tasks and duties led physicians to involve their patients in such activities as agriculture, weaving, working with animals, and sewing. Over time, this practice became quite common, and the conditions of many patients were improved.

Occupational therapy as we know it today had its beginning after World War I. The need to help disabled veterans of that war, and years later the veterans of World War II, stimulated the growth of this field. Even though its inception was in the psychiatric field, occupational therapy has developed an equally important role in other medical fields, including rehabilitation of physically disabled patients.

As more health care providers began to incorporate occupational therapy into their treatment philosophy, demand arose for workers who could assist occupational therapists with rehabilitation and office support services. Thus, the careers of occupational therapy assistant and occupational therapy aide were born. These health care professionals, who work under the direct supervision of occupational therapists, play an integral role in the care of people with mental, physical, developmental, or emotional limitations.

THE JOB

Occupational therapy is used to help provide rehabilitation services to persons with mental, physical, emotional, or developmental disabilities. The goal of occupational therapy is to improve a patient's quality of life by compensating for limitations caused by age, illness, or injury. It differs from physical therapy because it focuses not only on physical rehabilitation, but also on psychological well-being. Occupational therapy emphasizes improvement of the activities of daily living—including such functions as personal hygiene, dressing, eating, and cooking.

Occupational therapy assistants, under the supervision of the therapist, implement patient care plans and activities. They help patients improve mobility and productivity using a variety of activities and exercises. They may use adaptive techniques and equipment to help patients perform tasks many take for granted. A reacher, a long-handled device that pinches and grabs small items, may be used to pick up keys from the floor or a book from the shelf. Therapy assistants may have patients mix ingredients for a cake or flip a grilled cheese sandwich using a special spatula. Activities such as dancing, playing cards, or throwing a ball are fun, yet they help improve mobility and give the patients a sense of self-esteem. Therapists evaluate an activity, minimize the number of steps, and streamline movement so the patient will be less fatigued.

Assistants may also help therapists evaluate a patient's progress, change care plans as needed, make therapy appointments, and complete paperwork.

Occupational therapy aides are responsible for materials and equipment used during therapy. They assemble and clean equipment and make certain the therapists and assistants have what they need for a patient's therapy session. A therapy aide's duties are more clerical in nature. They answer telephones, schedule appointments, order supplies and equipment, and complete insurance forms and other paperwork.

REQUIREMENTS

High School

According to the U.S. Department of Labor, most occupational therapy aides receive on-the-job training, while occupational therapy assistants require further education after high school. For either position, however, a high school diploma is a must. Prepare for these careers by taking classes in biology, health, and social sciences. Anyone interested in doing this work must also be able to communicate clearly, follow directions, and work as part of a team. English or communication classes can help you improve on these skills.

In addition, admissions officers at postsecondary programs are favorably impressed if you have experience in the health care field. If you cannot find a paid job, consider volunteering at a local hospital or nursing home during your high school years.

Postsecondary Training

While occupational therapy aides receive on-the-job training, occupational therapy assistants must have either an associate's degree or certificate from an accredited OTA program. Programs are accredited by the Accreditation Council for Occupational Therapy Education (ACOTE), which is part of the American Occupational Therapy Association (AOTA). Approximately 135 programs are fully accredited by the ACOTE; in addition, a number of programs were on "inactive status," meaning that they were not currently accepting new students but may reactivate (begin accepting students again) in the future. A full listing of programs, as well as their contact information, is available by visiting http://www.aota.org/Students/Schools.aspx.

Generally, programs take two years to complete. Studies include courses such as human anatomy, psychology of adjustment, biology, human kinesiology, therapeutic media, and techniques. Most schools also require their students to take general classes as well to round out their education. These may be courses such as English, business math, and management. In addition to class work, you will be required to complete a period of supervised fieldwork, which will give you hands-on experience with occupational therapy.

Certification or Licensing

Occupational therapy assistants must pass the certifying test of the National Board for Certification in Occupational Therapy. After passing this test, assistants receive the designation certified occupational therapy assistant. Licensure requirements for assistants vary by state, so you will need to check with the licensing board of the state in which you want to work for specific information. Occupational therapy aides do not require certification or licensing.

Other Requirements

Occupational therapy assistants and aides must be able to take directions. OTAs should have a pleasant disposition, strong people skills, and a desire to help those in need. Assistants must also be patient and responsible. Aides, too, should be responsible. They also need to be detail oriented in order to keep track of paperwork and equipment. It is important for assistants and aides to work well as a team.

EXPLORING

A visit to your local hospital's occupational therapy department is the best way to learn about this field. Speak with occupational therapists, assistants, and aides to gain an understanding of the work they do. Also, the AOTA and other related organizations might be able to provide career information. School guidance and job centers, and the library, are good information sources.

EMPLOYERS

There are approximately 21,000 occupational therapy assistants and 5,400 occupational therapy aides employed in the United States. Approximately 30 percent of all assistants and aides work in a hospital setting, 23 percent are employed by offices of physicians and occupational therapists, and 18 percent work in nursing facilities. Others work in community care facilities for the elderly, home health care services, outpatient rehabilitation centers, and state government agencies.

STARTING OUT

The career services department of your local community college or technical school can provide a listing of jobs available in the occupational therapy field. Job openings are usually posted in hospital human resource departments. Professional groups are also a good source of information; for example, the AOTA's Web site has an employment page for members.

ADVANCEMENT

After some experience, occupational therapy assistants can be promoted to *lead assistant*. Lead assistants are responsible for making work schedules of other assistants and for the training of occupational therapy students. Since occupational therapy assistants work under the supervision of an occupational therapist, there is little room for advancement. Aides may return to school and train to become occupational therapy assistants. Some assistants and aides return to school to become occupational therapists. Some shift to other health care careers.

EARNINGS

According to the U.S. Department of Labor, the median yearly income of occupational therapy assistants was $42,060 in 2006. Salaries ranged from less than $26,050 to $58,270 or more annually. Naturally, experience, location, and type of employer all factor into the salaries paid.

The importance of education, though, cannot be overlooked, as assistants tend to earn more than aides. Median annual earnings of occupational therapist aides were $25,020 in 2006, according to the U.S. Department of Labor. Salaries ranged from less than $17,060 to $44,130 or more annually.

Benefits for full-time workers depend on the employer. They generally include health and life insurance, paid sick and vacation time, holiday pay, and a retirement plan.

WORK ENVIRONMENT

Most occupational therapy assistants and aides work during the day, although depending on the place of employment, some evening or weekend work may be required. Most therapy is done in a hospital or clinic setting that is clean, well lighted, and generally comfortable.

Occupational therapy assistants often use everyday items, settings, and activities to help rehabilitate their patients. Such props include kitchen settings, card games, dancing, or exercises. Therapy assistants should be in good physical shape, since heavy lifting—of patients as well as equipment—is a daily part of the job. Therapy assistants should also have stamina, since they are on their feet for much of the day.

OUTLOOK

According to the *Occupational Outlook Handbook*, employment for occupational therapy assistants and aides will grow much faster than the average for all occupations through 2014. However, only a small number of new jobs will actually be available due to the size of these occupations. Occupational growth will stem from an increased number of people with disabilities and elderly people. Although more people are living well into their 70s, 80s, and in some cases, 90s, they often need the kinds of services occupational therapy provides. Medical technology has greatly improved, saving many lives that in the past would be lost through accidents, stroke, or other illnesses. Such people need rehabilitation therapy as they recuperate. Hospitals and employers are hiring more therapy assistants to help with the workload and to reduce costs.

FOR MORE INFORMATION

For additional information on careers, education, and news related to the field, contact

American Occupational Therapy Association
4720 Montgomery Lane
PO Box 31220
Bethesda, MD 20824-1220
Tel: 301-652-2682
http://www.aota.org

For information on certification, contact

National Board for Certification in Occupational Therapy
Eugene B. Casey Building
800 South Frederick Avenue, Suite 200
Gaithersburg, MD 20877-4150
Tel: 301-990-7979
http://www.nbcot.org

Orientation and Mobility Specialists

OVERVIEW

Orientation and mobility specialists help people with disabilities stay actively involved in society. They teach blind, visually impaired, and individuals with disabilities how to master the skills necessary to live independently and often encourage them to participate in various educational or recreational programs. Specialists also serve as a source of information, referring clients to financial aid, benefits, and legal advice. These workers may be employed directly by an individual or indirectly through community planning, research, and publicity projects.

HISTORY

Helping those with disabilities has long been a part of the social work profession. As early as 1657, facilities called almshouses provided shelter, food, and work to the poor and those with disabilities. In the mid-1800s, middle-class women referred to as "friendly visitors" visited the homes of poor families to instruct people with disabilities in household management, the pursuit of employment, and the education of children. However, these friendly visitors and other early charitable organizations were sometimes limited in whom they would serve, often providing help and information only to those with their same moral views and religious backgrounds.

People with severe disabilities were often confined to institutions. By the late 18th century, many states and counties had built these facilities, then referred to as insane asylums, for the 24-hour care of

QUICK FACTS

School Subjects
Health
Psychology

Personal Skills
Communication/ideas
Helping/teaching

Work Environment
Primarily indoors
Primarily multiple locations

Minimum Education Level
Bachelor's degree

Salary Range
$27,280 to $43,040 to
$64,070+

Certification or Licensing
Required by certain states

Outlook
Faster than the average

DOT
076

GOE
14.06.01

NOC
4215

O*NET-SOC
N/A

people suffering from afflictions ranging from mental retardation to paralysis. The patients of these hospitals were often committed against their will by relatives. Few efforts were made to help patients return to society to lead normal, active lives.

The settlement houses of the late 19th century, such as Jane Addams's Hull House of Chicago, led to the development of more sensitive and enlightened ways to help people. Social workers lived among the residents, listening and learning along with them. But even with this new understanding of social work, those with disabilities were still unable to get complete assistance. Society wanted to help those in need but didn't necessarily want to live among them. As a result, separate schools, workplaces, and agencies for the disabled were established. Although social workers instructed blind people in how to cook and clean, how to use a guide dog, and how to read Braille, they made few efforts to integrate them into the community.

Legal efforts to end this discrimination began in 1920 with the passing of the Vocational Rehabilitation Act. This act led to the development of state and federal agencies focused on enhancing the employment opportunities for people with disabilities. Over the years, this act has broadened to include job counseling and retraining services and the provision of prosthetic and other assisting devices. More recent efforts toward ending discrimination in employment and public services include the passing of the Americans with Disabilities Act of 1990.

THE JOB

Although he was diagnosed with multiple sclerosis years ago, Ken Smith has only recently required the use of a wheelchair. He also has only partial use of his right hand. For the last few years, he has worked as a newspaper journalist, driving himself to crime scenes, taking notes during interviews, and writing at a frantic pace to keep up with the pace of the newsroom. Now that he requires a wheelchair to get around, he is going to have to make many adjustments in his life. Fortunately for Smith, there are a number of services and benefits to help him; he just needs to know how to find this help.

The simple act of providing information is one of the most important jobs of an orientation and mobility specialist. These workers help to direct people like Smith to the many agencies available that assist those with vision and mobility impairments. By listening carefully to the problem, orientation and mobility specialists determine the best route for assistance, contact the agency on behalf of the client, and make sure the client receives the proper assistance. Because of limited funding and support, disability services are often unable to promote themselves. The biggest problem facing communities is not the lack of services available, but the lack of public awareness of these outlets.

However, Smith will require much more than names and phone numbers from an orientation and mobility specialist. He not only needs to find the right wheelchair, but he also needs instruction on how to use it. His home needs to be analyzed to determine what modifications need to be made (for example, wheelchair ramps, handrails, and wider doorways). If the necessary modifications cannot be made, he will have to consider moving to a new place. For all of these somewhat daunting decisions, Smith can ask an orientation and mobility specialist for advice.

Smith's workplace may also require modifications. Though perfectly capable of continuing his work as a journalist, he is going to have to fulfill his duties in different ways. For example, a special car may be required. Because of the limited use of his hand, he may need a modified computer keyboard or an assistant. An orientation and mobility specialist can serve as a client's advocate, negotiating with employers to prevent any cause for discrimination in the workplace. Specialists may also offer training and education programs to integrate or reintegrate the client into the workplace.

An orientation and mobility specialist also serves as a counselor. A client may need individual therapy or a support group. The family of the client may also need counseling on how to adjust to a parent's or child's disability.

In addition to offering services that directly benefit the client (counseling, advocacy, education, and referral), some specialists may offer services that have indirect benefits for clients. These additional services include outreach, publicity, planning, and research. Because of a general lack of awareness of the social services available, orientation and mobility specialists may focus on ways to educate the public about the challenges facing those with disabilities. They may lead fund-raising efforts for research or programs aimed at assisting the disabled community.

REQUIREMENTS
High School
Because you will need a college degree and a well-rounded education, take your high school's program of college preparatory classes. These classes should include math and science courses as well as a foreign language. Strong communication skills are needed for this work, so to improve your skills in this area take four years of English. Speech and journalism classes are also beneficial.

Courses in history, social studies, sociology, and psychology are also recommended.

Because a large part of the job is providing information about disability services, you should be comfortable using the Internet and various computer programs. Not only will you have to be able to work with computers yourself, you may be required to teach clients how to use them, too.

Postsecondary Training

The Association for Education and Rehabilitation of the Blind and Visually Impaired (commonly known as AER) provides a listing of approved orientation and mobility programs at the graduate, under-graduate, and certification-only levels. Programs include instruction in mobility techniques, where students simulate blindness or limited vision with blindfolds or other devices. Internships with disability agencies are also incorporated into the programs.

Other specialists prepare themselves for the career by studying social work. The Council on Social Work Education requires that five areas be covered in accredited bachelor's degree social work pro-grams: human behavior and the social environment, social welfare policy and services, social work practice, research, and field practi-cum. Most programs require two years of liberal arts study, followed by two years of study in the social work major. Also, students must complete a field practicum of at least 400 hours.

Though some starting positions require only a bachelor's degree, most supervisory and administrative positions within social work require further education. Graduate programs are organized accord-ing to fields of practice (e.g., mental health care), problem areas (e.g., substance abuse), population groups (e.g., the elderly), and prac-tice roles (e.g., practice with individuals, families, or communities). They are usually two-year programs with at least 900 hours of field practice. Doctoral degrees are also available for those interested in research, planning, or community outreach jobs.

Certification or Licensing

Only selected states require orientation and mobility specialists to be certified. The Academy for Certification of Vision Rehabilita-tion and Education Professionals offers certification for orientation and mobility specialists who meet certain educational and experi-ence requirements. To be eligible to sit for the certification exam, individuals must first complete an AER-approved orientation and mobility program. Applicants who meet these certification require-ments can use the designation *certified orientation and mobility specialist.*

Other Requirements

For years, people with disabilities have faced discrimination. This discrimination is fueled by fear, by misunderstanding, and by the way people with disabilities are represented in popular culture. Orientation and mobility specialists must be able to honestly address their own perceptions of people with disabilities. Specialists must be sensitive to the client's situation and have a genuine interest in involving that person in the community and workplace.

Specialists also work frequently with the elderly, which requires understanding the aging experience. Workers must be patient and be good listeners to provide the elderly with the supportive network they need.

Communication skills are also very important. Much of the work as an orientation and mobility specialist involves talking and listening to clients, teaching, interviewing, and counseling. You will need to provide clear instructions to clients, their families, and their employers.

Because many of the problems facing those with disabilities stem from discrimination, many specialists work to educate the public about living with disabilities through research, reports, and fundraising. Being comfortable talking to a variety of people and in a variety of settings is an asset for these specialists.

EXPLORING

To learn more about this work, you can explore Web sites concerning disabilities and social work. A job in the school or public library helping people conduct research will put your information retrieval skills to good use. Working on the school newspaper will also help you develop your writing, researching, and interviewing skills, all important aspects of social work.

Part-time data entry jobs at a hospital or long-term care facility can familiarize you with medical terminology and the services available to people with disabilities. A part-time job in a retail pharmacy will involve you directly with people with disabilities and also the services that pay for the rental and purchase of wheelchairs, walkers, and canes. You can also gain experience by volunteering at any social service agency to get a sense of the work environment and responsibilities.

EMPLOYERS

Orientation and mobility specialists can find work with for-profit, nonprofit, and public programs. They may work in hospitals and community agencies such as transitional living services or with private agencies that focus on providing services specifically to those with disabilities.

An orientation and mobility specialist may also be self-employed, providing service on a contract basis to individuals or social service agencies.

STARTING OUT

To gain experience in social work, consider working with a social service agency specializing in information and referral. Rehabilitation centers, senior homes, schools, and summer camps for the blind, visually impaired, and disabled also offer many opportunities for experience. Because of limited funding, staffing may consist of only a few social work professionals, and the rest may be volunteers or assistants. Volunteer work may lead to full-time employment or simply introduce you to other social work professionals who can provide career guidance and letters of reference.

ADVANCEMENT

Orientation and mobility specialists may advance to become supervisors of assistants or executive directors of rehabilitation agencies. Another possible route for advancement is through teaching.

The more challenging and better-paying jobs tend to go to those with more years of practical experience and higher degrees. Further study, extensive experience, and good references will lead to advancement in the profession. Also, many social work programs offer continuing education workshops, courses, and seminars. These refresher courses help practicing specialists refine their skills and learn about new areas of practice, methods, and problems. These courses are intended to supplement previous education, not substitute for a bachelor's or master's degree. Continuing education can lead to job promotions and salary increases.

EARNINGS

The higher the degree held by specialists, the higher their earning potential. Those with a Ph.D. can take jobs in indirect service, research, and planning. Salaries also vary among regions; in general, social workers on the East and West Coasts earn higher salaries than those in the Midwest. During the first five years of practice, salaries increase faster than in later years.

Medical and public health social workers earned a median annual salary of $43,040 in 2006, according to the U.S. Department of

Labor. The lowest paid 10 percent earned less than $27,280 and the highest paid 10 percent earned more than $64,070.

Specialists who work in school systems are generally paid on the same scale as teachers in the system. Those who work for private clients are usually paid by the hour or per session.

WORK ENVIRONMENT

Orientation and mobility specialists work part of the time in an office, analyzing and updating client files, interviewing clients over the phone, and talking with other service agencies. Depending on the size of the agency, office duties such as typing letters, filing, and answering phones may be performed by an aide or volunteer.

The rest of their time is spent outside the office, interacting directly with clients and others. Orientation and mobility specialists are involved directly with the people they serve and must carefully examine their clients' living conditions and family relations.

Advocacy involves work in a variety of different environments; it involves meetings with clients' employers, agency directors, and local legislators. Should the client press charges for discrimination, orientation and mobility specialists may be called upon to testify in court.

Both counseling and advocacy can be stressful aspects of the work, but helping to empower people with disabilities can be very rewarding.

OUTLOOK

According to the American Association of People with Disabilities, more than 56 million people (nearly one out of every five Americans) have a disability. In addition to continuing the fight against discrimination in the workplace and in general society, those with disabilities also need assistance in order to live productive lives.

Future funding is an important consideration for social service agencies. In many cases, the agencies providing information and referral must compete for funding with the very programs to which they refer people. This calls for good relationships between agencies and services. In order for agencies to receive adequate funding, social workers, including orientation and mobility specialists, must conduct research and provide reports to federal, state, and local governments showing proof of financial need. Their reports help to illustrate where funds should be allocated to best serve the disabled community.

According to the U.S. Department of Labor, the employment of social workers, including those that work with the visually and physically impaired, is expected to increase faster than the average for all occupations through 2014. Specialists will continue to increase public awareness of the importance of aid for those with disabilities and the visually impaired. Assistance services will continue to make their way into more public areas, such as libraries, workplaces, and other public facilities.

New computer technology will continue to cater to the special needs of the disabled. The development of specialized equipment and the expansion of Internet resources allow those with disabilities and the visually impaired to access online resources for assistance. Orientation and mobility specialists will be needed to help those with disabilities use new technology to their best advantage.

FOR MORE INFORMATION

For information on certification, contact
Academy for Certification of Vision Rehabilitation and Education Professionals
3333 North Campbell Avenue, Suite 11
Tucson, AZ 85719-2362
Tel: 520-887-6816
Email: info@acvrep.org
http://www.acvrep.org

For resources and advocacy for people with disabilities, contact
American Association of People with Disabilities
1629 K Street, NW, Suite 503
Washington, DC 20006-1634
Tel: 800-840-8844
http://www.aapd.com

For information on educational programs, contact
Association for Education and Rehabilitation of the Blind and Visually Impaired
1703 North Beauregard Street, Suite 440
Alexandria, VA 22311-1744
Tel: 703-671-4500
http://www.aerbvi.org

To read frequently asked questions about how to become a social worker, check out the following Web site:
Council on Social Work Education
1725 Duke Street, Suite 500
Alexandria, VA 22314-3457

Tel: 703-683-8080
Email: info@cswe.org
http://www.cswe.org

For information about careers, education, and job leads, contact
National Association of Social Workers
750 First Street, NE, Suite 700
Washington, DC 20002-4241
Tel: 202-408-8600
http://www.socialworkers.org

For career information and job listings available in Canada, contact
Canadian Association of Social Workers
383 Parkdale Avenue, Suite 402
Ottawa, ON K1Y 4R4 Canada
Tel: 613-729-6668
http://www.casw-acts.ca

Physical Therapists

OVERVIEW

Physical therapists, formerly called *physiotherapists*, are health care specialists who restore mobility, alleviate pain and suffering, and work to prevent permanent disability for their patients. They test and measure the functions of the musculoskeletal, neurological, pulmonary, and cardiovascular systems and treat problems in these systems caused by illness, injury, or birth defect. Physical therapists provide preventive, restorative, and rehabilitative treatment for their patients. Approximately 155,000 physical therapists are licensed to practice in the United States.

HISTORY

The practice of physical therapy has developed as our knowledge of medicine and our understanding of the functions of the human body have grown. During the first part of the 20th century, there were tremendous strides in medical practice in general. The wartime experiences of medical teams who had to rehabilitate seriously injured soldiers contributed to the medical use and acceptance of physical therapy practices. The polio epidemic in the 1940s, which left many victims paralyzed, also led to the demand for improved physical therapy.

A professional association was organized in 1921, and physical therapy began to achieve professional stature. The American Physical Therapy Association (APTA) now serves a membership of more than 71,000 physical therapists, physical therapy assistants, and students.

Today the use of physical therapy has expanded beyond hospitals, where it has been traditionally practiced. Physical therapists now work in private practices, nursing homes, sports facilities, home health agencies, public and private schools, academic institutions, hospices, and in industrial physical therapy programs, a reflection of their versatility of skills and the public's need for comprehensive health care.

THE JOB

To initiate a program of physical therapy, the physical therapist consults the individual's medical history, examines the patient and identifies problems, confers with the physician or other health care professionals involved in the patient's care, establishes objectives and treatment goals that are consistent with the patient's needs, and determines the methods for accomplishing the objectives.

Treatment goals established by the physical therapist include preventing disability, relieving pain, and restoring function. In the presence of illness or injury, the ultimate goal is to assist the patient's physical recovery and reentry into the community, home, and work environment at the highest level of independence and self-sufficiency possible.

To aid and maintain recovery, the physical therapist also provides education to involve patients in their own care. The educational program may include exercises, posture reeducation, and relaxation practices. In many cases, the patient's family is involved in the educational program to provide emotional support or physical assistance as needed. These activities evolve into a continuum of self-care when the patient is discharged from the physical therapy program.

Physical therapists provide care for many types of patients of all ages. This includes working with burn victims to prevent abnormal scarring and loss of movement, with stroke victims to regain movement

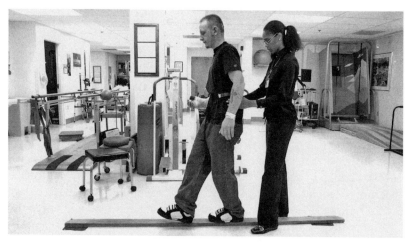

A physical therapist helps a soldier injured during the Iraq War regain his balancing skills. (Norbert von der Groeben, The Image Works)

and independent living, with cancer patients to relieve discomfort, and with cardiac patients to improve endurance and achieve independence. Physical therapists also provide preventive exercise programs, postural improvement, and physical conditioning to individuals who perceive the need to promote their own health and well-being.

Physical therapists should have a creative approach to their work. No two patients respond the same way to exactly the same kind of treatment. The challenge is to find the right way to encourage the patient to make progress, to respond to treatment, to feel a sense of achievement, and to refuse to become discouraged if progress is slow.

Many physical therapists acquire specialized knowledge through clinical experience and educational preparation in specialty areas of practice, such as cardiopulmonary physical therapy, clinical electrophysiologic physical therapy, neurologic physical therapy, orthopedic physical therapy, pediatric physical therapy, geriatric physical therapy, and sports physical therapy.

REQUIREMENTS
High School
While you are in high school you can begin to prepare for this career by taking college preparatory classes. These should include biology, chemistry, physics, health, and mathematics. Because so much of this work involves direct contact with clients, you should improve your people skills as well as your communication skills by taking psychology, sociology, and English classes. Also, take computer science courses so that you are computer literate. Statistics, history, and a foreign language are also beneficial.

Postsecondary Training
Physical therapists attain their professional skills through extensive education that takes place both in the classroom and in clinical settings. You should attend a school accredited by the Commission on Accreditation in Physical Therapy Education (CAPTE) to receive the most thorough education. CAPTE now only accredits schools offering postbaccalaureate degrees (master's and doctorate degrees), and you will need one of these degrees to practice physical therapy. Previously, CAPTE had accredited bachelor's degree programs; however, this change was made to give students an appropriate amount of time to study liberal arts as well as a physical therapy curriculum. Course work should include classes in the humanities as well as those geared for the profession, such as anatomy, human growth and development, and therapeutic procedures. Clinical experience is done as supervised fieldwork in such settings as hospitals, home care agencies, and nursing homes. According to the APTA, there are 199

accredited academic institutions supporting 31 master's programs and 179 doctoral programs. Visit the APTA's Web site (http://www .apta.org) for a list of accredited programs.

Certification or Licensing

Specialist certification of physical therapists, while not a requirement for employment, is a desirable advanced credential. The American Board of Physical Therapy Specialties, an appointed group of the American Physical Therapy Association, certifies physical therapists who demonstrate specialized knowledge and advanced clinical proficiency in a specialty area of physical therapy practice and who pass a certifying examination. The seven areas of specialization are cardiopulmonary, clinical electrophysiologic, neurologic, orthopedics, pediatrics, geriatrics, and sports.

Upon graduating from an accredited physical therapy educational program, all physical therapists must successfully complete a national examination. Other licensing requirements vary by state. You will need to check with the licensing board of the state in which you hope to work for specific information.

Other Requirements

Successful physical therapists enjoy working with people and helping others to feel better, both physically and emotionally. They need creativity and patience to determine a treatment plan for each client and to help them achieve treatment goals. Physical therapists must also be committed to lifelong learning because new developments in technology and medicine mean that therapists must continually update their knowledge. It is also a plus to have a positive attitude and an outgoing personality.

EXPLORING

Your first step in exploring this field could be to talk with a physical therapist in your community about the work. Your school guidance counselor should be able to help you arrange for such an informational interview. Hands-on experience is important to get because schools that you apply to will take this into consideration. This experience will also help you decide how well you like working with people who are sometimes in pain or confused. One possibility is to volunteer at a physical therapy program. If such an opening is not available, try volunteering at a local hospital, nursing home, or other care facility to gain experience working in these settings. You can also look for volunteer opportunities or summer jobs at camps for people with disabilities. Paid part-time positions may also be available as a hospital orderly or aide to a physical therapist.

EMPLOYERS

Hospitals employ nearly 60 percent of physical therapists. According to the U.S. Department of Labor, the rest work in settings such as offices of physicians, private physical therapy offices, community health centers, sports facilities, nursing homes, and schools. Physical therapists may be involved in research or teach at colleges and universities. Veterans Administration hospitals and other government agencies also hire physical therapists. Some physical therapists are self-employed. Approximately 155,000 physical therapists are employed in the United States.

STARTING OUT

Physical therapy graduates may obtain jobs through their college career services offices or by answering ads in any of a variety of professional journals. They can apply in person or send letters and resumes to hospitals, medical centers, rehabilitation facilities, and other places that hire physical therapists. Some find jobs through the APTA.

ADVANCEMENT

In a hospital or other health care facility, one may rise from being a staff physical therapist to being the chief physical therapist and then

Books to Read

American Physical Therapy Association. *Guide to Physical Therapist Practice.* 2d ed., revised. Alexandria, Va.: American Physical Therapy Association, 2001.

Campbell, Suzann K., Robert J. Palisano, and Darl W. Vander Linden. *Physical Therapy for Children.* 3d ed. Philadelphia: W.B. Saunders, 2005.

Esterson, Samuel H. *Starting and Managing Your Own Physical Therapy Practice.* Sudbury, Mass.: Jones and Bartlett Publishers, 2004.

Goodman, Catherine Cavallaro, et al. *Pathology: Implications for the Physical Therapist.* 2d ed. Philadelphia: W.B. Saunders, 2002.

Nosse, Larry J., et al. *Managerial and Supervisory Principles for Physical Therapists.* 2d ed. Philadelphia: Lippincott Williams & Wilkins, 2004.

Page, Catherine G., and Laura Lee Swisher. *Professionalism in Physical Therapy: History, Practice, and Development.* Philadelphia: W.B. Saunders, 2005.

Pagliarulo, Michael A. *Introduction to Physical Therapy.* 3d ed. St. Louis: C.V. Mosby, 2006.

director of the department. Administrative responsibilities are usually given to those physical therapists who have had several years of experience plus the personal qualities that prepare them for undertaking this kind of assignment.

After working in a hospital or other institution for several years, some physical therapists open up their own practices or go into a group practice, with both often paying higher salaries.

EARNINGS

Salaries for physical therapists depend on experience and type of employer. Physical therapists earned an annual average salary of $66,200 in 2006, according to the U.S. Department of Labor. On average, 50 percent earned between $55,030 and $78,080; the top paid 10 percent earned $94,810 or more a year. In 2006, the top paying industries for physical therapists were: child day care services, $81,310; home health care services, $75,670; employment services, $69,290; and nursing care facilities, $68,870.

Salaried physical therapists also enjoy fringe benefits such as paid vacation, 401(k) savings plans, and medical and dental insurance.

WORK ENVIRONMENT

The typical physical therapist works approximately 40 hours each week, including Saturdays. Patient sessions may be brief or may last an hour or more. Usually, treatment is on an individual basis, but occasionally therapy may be given in groups when the patients' problems are similar.

OUTLOOK

Employment for physical therapists is expected to grow much faster than the average for all occupations through 2014, according to the U.S. Department of Labor. One reason for this strong growth is the fact that the median age of the American population is rising, and this older demographic group develops a higher number of medical conditions that cause physical pain and disability. Also, advances in medical technology save more people, who then require physical therapy. For example, as more trauma victims and newborns with birth defects survive, the need for physical therapists will rise. Another reason is the public's growing interest in physical fitness, which has resulted in an increasing number of athletic injuries requiring physical therapy. In industry and fitness centers, a growing interest in pain and injury prevention also has created new opportunities for physical therapists.

Employment prospects for physical therapists should continue to be excellent into the next decade—especially in acute hospital, rehabilitation, and orthopedic settings. If enrollment in accredited physical therapy programs remains at the current level, there will be more openings for physical therapists than qualified individuals to fill them.

FOR MORE INFORMATION
The APTA offers the brochure Your Career In Physical Therapy, *a directory of accredited schools, certification, and general career information.*

American Physical Therapy Association (APTA)
1111 North Fairfax Street
Alexandria, VA 22314-1488
Tel: 800-999-2782
http://www.apta.org

For information on accredited programs, contact
Commission on Accreditation in Physical Therapy Education
Email: accreditation@apta.org
http://www.apta.org/CAPTE

INTERVIEW

Angela Wilson Pennisi is the president of Lakeshore Sports Physical Therapy in Chicago, Illinois. She has been a physical therapist for more than 10 years. Angela discussed the field with the editors of Careers in Focus: Therapists.

Q. Please tell us about your practice.
A. I opened Lakeshore Sports Physical Therapy in 2000. I serve as director for the practice and continue to evaluate and treat patients on a daily basis. Four additional physical therapists work in my practice. I also serve as president for a second company, Physioview. Physioview.com is a Web site that provides exercise instructional materials to physical therapists and their patients.

Q. Why did you decide to enter this career?
A. As a college sophomore, I was considering two basic career paths. I had an interest in health, education, and fitness and also in Spanish language and community services. I worked with a career counselor to discuss these two seemingly different options. He reassured me that I would be able to handle the science coursework required for physical therapy, which

was my major concern. Though I was an excellent student, my strengths were in English, writing, and creative subjects. However, as I initiated courses in biology, chemistry, and physics, I realized the benefits of pushing myself to take courses that were challenging to me. I may not have been the best student in the class, but with work, I earned good marks. While my interest in Spanish seemed to conflict at the time, I have also utilized my language education regularly as a physical therapist.

Q. **How did you train for this career? What was your educational path?**

A. I completed a bachelor of arts degree at the University of Nebraska–Lincoln. My major was in history because I wanted to complete a degree in another unrelated area of interest. Since I had to take many science courses in order to apply to a physical therapy program, my undergraduate degree also included minors in biology and psychology. I was accepted to my physical therapy program of choice at Columbia University in New York. I graduated with honors from a two-year master's program in physical therapy.

Q. **Did you participate in an internship as part of your training?**

A. My program required three clinical affiliations. Each affiliation lasted six to eight weeks. My first internship was in the outpatient physical therapy department at a city hospital in New York City. I also completed an affiliation with Columbia-Presbyterian Medical Center, seeing patients with brain tumors, multiple sclerosis, and other neurological disorders. My final affiliation was at a pediatric hospital in Providence, Rhode Island. In each affiliation, I worked with the assistance of and under the supervision of a licensed physical therapist. I had to meet certain clinical criteria and competencies in order to pass each affiliation.

Q. **What advice would you give to high school students who are interested in the field?**

A. Spend time observing a physical therapist who works for a therapist-owned practice. Observing in such an environment will allow an interested student to see the potential rewards and opportunities available when working in a "gold-standard" practice. I also recommend that the student observe other health professionals, such as physicians, nurses, physician assistants, speech therapists, and occupational therapists, to be sure that he or she is choosing the field that fits the best.

Physical Therapy Assistants

OVERVIEW

Physical therapy assistants help to restore physical function in people with injury, birth defects, or disease. They assist physical therapists with a variety of techniques, such as exercise, massage, heat, and water therapy.

Physical therapy assistants work directly under the supervision of physical therapists. They teach and help patients improve functional activities required in their daily lives, such as walking, climbing, and moving from one place to another. The assistants observe patients during treatments, record the patients' responses and progress, and report these to the physical therapist, either orally or in writing. They fit patients for and teach them to use braces, artificial limbs, crutches, canes, walkers, wheelchairs, and other devices. They may make physical measurements to assess the effects of treatments or to evaluate patients' range of motion, length and girth of body parts, and vital signs. Physical therapy assistants act as members of a team and regularly confer with other members of the physical therapy staff. There are approximately 59,000 physical therapy assistants employed in the United States.

HISTORY

The practice of treating ailments with heat and exercise is very old. For many centuries, people have known of the therapeutic value of hot baths, sunlight, and massage. The ancient Greeks and the Romans used these methods, and there is a long tradition of them in the far northern part of Europe.

Two factors spurred the development of physical therapy techniques during this century: the world wars and epidemic poliomyelitis. These catastrophes created large numbers of young but seriously disabled patients.

World War I brought about great strides in medicine and in our understanding of how the human body functions. Among these was the realization that physical therapy could help shorten the recovery time of the wounded. A Reconstruction Aide corps in the U.S. Army was organized to perform physical therapy in military hospitals, and the army organized the first department of physical therapy in 1916. Training programs were hastily started to teach physiotherapy, as physical therapy used to be called, to those administering services.

The American Physical Therapy Association was organized in 1921, thus establishing physical therapy's professional stature. In 1925, the association took on the responsibility of identifying approved training programs for physical therapy personnel.

During World War II, physical therapy's benefits were recognized. Because medical teams in the armed forces were able to rehabilitate seriously injured patients, this field gained acceptance from the medical world.

Between the wars, polio became a major health problem, especially because it left many of its victims paralyzed. In 1944, the United States suffered the worst polio epidemic in its history. Public demand for improved physical therapy services led to more therapists and improved techniques. As knowledge grew and the number of people in the field grew, physical therapy services were redefined and expanded in scope. Physical therapy is now available in many settings outside the hospital. Currently there is preventive musculoskeletal screening for children in pediatric clinics and public schools, therapy in industrial settings for workers recovering from injuries on the job, therapy for the elderly in nursing homes and in community health agencies, and therapy for people with athletic injuries in sports medicine clinics.

The physical therapy assistant's occupation is rather new. It was developed in 1967 to help meet this greatly expanded interest in physical therapy services. Physical therapy assistants and physical therapy aides (another new occupational category, requiring less education than an assistant) specialize in some of the less complex treatments that were formerly administered by the physical therapist.

THE JOB

Physical therapy personnel work to prevent, diagnose, and rehabilitate, to restore physical function, prevent permanent disability as much as possible, and help people achieve their maximum attainable performance. For many patients, this objective involves daily living skills, such as eating, grooming, dressing, bathing, and other basic movements that unimpaired people do automatically without thinking.

Physical therapy may alleviate conditions such as muscular pain, spasm, and weakness, joint pain and stiffness, and neuromuscular incoordination. These conditions may be caused by any number of disorders, including fractures, burns, amputations, arthritis, nerve or muscular injuries, trauma, birth defects, stroke, multiple sclerosis, and cerebral palsy. Patients of all ages receive physical therapy services; they may have severe disabilities or they may need only minimal therapeutic intervention.

Physical therapy assistants always work under the direction of a qualified physical therapist. Other members of the health team may be a physician or surgeon, nurse, occupational therapist, psychologist, or vocational counselor. Each of these practitioners helps establish and achieve realistic goals consistent with the patient's individual needs. Physical therapy assistants help perform tests to evaluate disabilities and determine the most suitable treatment for the patient; then, as the treatment progresses, they routinely report the patient's condition to the physical therapist. If they observe a patient having serious problems during treatment, the assistants notify the therapist as soon as possible. Physical therapy assistants generally perform complicated therapeutic procedures decided by the physical therapist; however, assistants may initiate routine procedures independently.

These procedures may include physical exercises, which are the most varied and widely used physical treatments. Exercises may be simple or complicated, easy or strenuous, active or passive. Active motions are performed by the patient alone and strengthen or train muscles. Passive exercises involve the assistant moving the body part through the motion, which improves mobility of the joint but does not strengthen muscle. For example, for a patient with a fractured arm, both active and passive exercise may be appropriate. The passive exercises may be designed to maintain or increase the range of motion in the shoulder, elbow, wrist, and finger joints, while active resistive exercises strengthen muscles weakened by disuse. An elderly patient who has suffered a stroke may need guided exercises aimed at keeping the joints mobile, regaining the function of a limb, walking, or climbing stairs. A child with cerebral palsy who would otherwise never walk may be helped to learn coordination exercises that enable crawling, sitting balance, standing balance, and, finally, walking.

Patients sometimes perform exercises in bed or immersed in warm water. Besides its usefulness in alleviating stiffness or paralysis, exercise

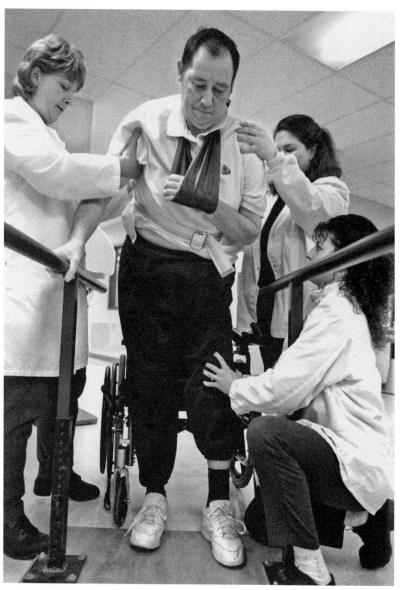

Physical therapy professionals help a man, who is recovering from a brain hemorrhage, during a physical therapy session. *(Syracuse Newspapers/ The Image Works)*

also helps to improve circulation, relax tense muscles, correct posture, and aid the breathing of patients with lung problems.

Other treatments that physical therapy assistants may administer include massages, traction for patients with neck or back pain, ultrasound and various kinds of heat treatment for diseases such as arthritis that inflame joints or nerves, cold applications to reduce swelling, pain, or hemorrhaging, and ultraviolet light.

Physical therapy assistants train patients to manage devices and equipment that they either need temporarily or permanently. For example, they instruct patients how to walk with canes or crutches using proper gait or how to maneuver well in a wheelchair. They also teach patients how to apply, remove, care for, and cope with splints, braces, and artificial body parts.

Physical therapy personnel must often work on improving the emotional state of patients, preparing them psychologically for treatments. The overwhelming sense of hopelessness and lack of confidence that afflict many patients with disabilities can reduce the patients' success in achieving improved functioning. The health team must be attuned to both the physical and nonphysical aspects of patients to assure that treatments are most beneficial. Sometimes physical therapy personnel work with patients' families to educate them on how to provide simple physical treatments and psychological support at home.

In addition, physical therapy assistants may perform office duties: They schedule patients, keep records, handle inventory, and order supplies. These duties may also be handled by *physical therapy aides*.

REQUIREMENTS

High School

Does this work sound interesting to you? If so, you can prepare for it while still in high school by taking biology, health, and mathematics classes. Psychology, sociology, and even social studies classes will be helpful, because they will give you an understanding of people. And, since you will be working so closely with clients as well as other professionals, you will need excellent communication skills. Therefore, take English courses and other classes that will improve these skills, such as speech. It is also a good idea to take computer science classes since almost all employers require their employees to have computer communication skills.

Postsecondary Training

In order to do this work, you will need a degree from an accredited physical therapy assistant program. Accreditation is given by the Commission on Accreditation in Physical Therapy Education (CAPTE), which is part of the American Physical Therapy Association (APTA). These programs, leading to an associate's degree, are usually offered at community and junior colleges. Typically lasting two years, the programs combine academic instruction with a period of supervised clinical practice in a physical therapy setting. According to the APTA, there are 221 accredited schools offering assistant programs as well as 24 programs in development. Information about these programs can be found on the APTA's Web site, http://www.apta.org. The first year of study is typically taken up with general course work, while the second year is focused on professional classes. Classes you can expect to take include mathematics, biology, applied physical sciences, psychology, human growth and development, and physical therapist assistant procedures such as massage, therapeutic exercise, and heat and cold therapy.

In recent years, admission to accredited programs has been fairly competitive, with three to five applicants for each available opening.

Some physical therapy assistants begin their careers while in the armed forces, which operate training programs. While these programs are not sufficient for state licensure and do not award degrees, they can serve as an excellent introduction to the field for students who later enter more complete training programs.

Certification or Licensing

More than 40 states require regulation of physical therapy assistants in the form of registration, certification, or licensure. Typically, graduation from a CAPTE-accredited program and passing a written exam are needed for licensing. Because requirements vary by state, you will need to check with your state's licensure board for specific information.

Other Requirements

Physical therapy assistants must have stamina, patience, and determination, but at the same time they must be able to establish personal relationships quickly and successfully. They should genuinely like and understand people, both under normal conditions and under the stress of illness. An outgoing personality is highly desirable as is the ability to instill confidence and enthusiasm in patients. Much of the work of physical retraining and restoring is very repetitive, and assistants may not perceive any progress for long periods of time. At times patients may seem unable or unwilling to cooperate. In such cases, assistants need boundless patience, to appreciate small gains and build on them. When restoration to good health is not attainable, physical therapist assistants must help patients adjust to a different way of life and find ways to cope with their situation. Creativity is an asset in devising methods that help people with disabilities achieve greater self-sufficiency. Assistants should be flexible and open to suggestions offered by their coworkers and willing and able to follow directions closely.

Because the job can be physically demanding, physical therapy assistants must be reasonably strong and enjoy physical activity. Manual dexterity and good coordination are needed to adjust equipment and assist patients. Assistants should be able to lift, climb, stoop, and kneel.

EXPLORING

While still in high school, you can experience this work by getting summer or part-time employment or by volunteering in the physical therapy department of a hospital or clinic. Also, many schools, both public and private, have volunteer assistance programs for work with students with disabilities. You can also gain direct experience by working with children with disabilities in a summer camp.

These opportunities will provide you with direct job experience that will help you determine if you have the personal qualities necessary for this career. If you are unable to get direct experience, you should talk to a physical therapist or physical therapy assistant during career-day programs at your high school. It may also be possible for you to arrange to visit a physical therapy department, watch the staff at work, and ask questions.

EMPLOYERS

Physical therapy assistants are employed in hospitals, rehabilitation centers, schools for those with disabilities, nursing homes, community and government health agencies, physicians' or physical therapists' offices, and facilities for those with mental disabilities. There are approximately 59,000 physical therapy assistants employed in the United States.

STARTING OUT

One good way to find a job is to access the resources available at the career services office of your educational institution. Alternatively, you can apply to the physical therapy departments of local hospitals, rehabilitation centers, extended-care facilities, and other potential employers. Openings are listed in the classified ads of newspapers, professional journals, and with private and public employment agencies. In locales where training programs have produced many physical therapy assistants, competition for jobs may be keen. In such cases, you may want to widen your search to areas where there is less competition, especially suburban and rural areas.

ADVANCEMENT

With experience, physical therapy assistants are often given greater responsibility and better pay. In large health care facilities, supervisory possibilities may open up. In small institutions that employ only one physical therapist, the physical therapist assistant may eventually take care of all the technical tasks that go on in the department, within the limitations of his or her training and education.

Physical therapy assistants with degrees from accredited programs are generally in the best position to gain advancement in any setting. They sometimes decide to earn a postbaccalaureate degree in physical therapy and become fully qualified physical therapists.

EARNINGS

Salaries for physical therapy assistants vary considerably depending on geographical location, employer, and level of experience. Physical therapy assistants earned median annual salaries of $41,360 in 2006, according to the U.S. Department of Labor. The lowest paid 10 percent earned less than $26,190; the highest paid 10 percent earned more than $57,220.

Fringe benefits vary, although they usually include paid holidays and vacations, health insurance, and pension plans.

WORK ENVIRONMENT

Physical therapy is generally administered in pleasant, clean, well-lighted, and well-ventilated surroundings. The space devoted to physical therapy services is often large, in order to accommodate activities such as gait training and exercises and procedures requiring equipment. Some procedures are given at patients' bedsides.

In the physical therapy department, patients come and go all day, many in wheelchairs, on walkers, canes, crutches, or stretchers. The staff tries to maintain a purposeful, harmonious, congenial atmosphere as they and the patients work toward the common goal of restoring physical efficacy.

The work can be exhausting. Physical therapy assistants may be on their feet for hours at a time, and they may have to move heavy equipment, lift patients, and help them to stand and walk. Most assistants work daytime hours, five days a week, although some positions require evening or weekend work. Some assistants work on a part-time basis.

The combined physical and emotional demands of the job can exert a considerable strain. Prospective assistants would be wise to seek out some job experience related to physical therapy so that they have a practical understanding of their psychological and physical capacities. By exploring their suitability for the work, they can make a better commitment to the training program.

Job satisfaction can be great for physical therapy assistants as they can see how their efforts help to make people's lives much more rewarding.

OUTLOOK

Employment prospects are very good for physical therapy assistants; the U.S. Department of Labor predicts that employment will grow much faster than the average for all occupations through 2014. Many new positions for physical therapy assistants are expected to open up as hospital programs aiding people with disabilities expand, and as long-term care facilities seek to offer residents more adequate services.

A major contributing factor is the increasing number of Americans aged 65 and over. This group tends to suffer a disproportionate amount of the accidents and chronic illnesses that necessitate physical therapy services. Many from the baby boom generation are reaching the age common for heart attacks, thus creating a need for more cardiac and physical rehabilitation. Legislation that requires appropriate public education for children with disabilities also may increase the demand for physical therapy services. As more adults engage in strenuous physical exercise, more musculoskeletal injuries will result, thus increasing demand for physical therapy services.

FOR MORE INFORMATION

The APTA offers the brochure Your Career In Physical Therapy, *a directory of accredited schools, certification, and general career information.*

American Physical Therapy Association (APTA)
1111 North Fairfax Street
Alexandria, VA 22314-1488
Tel: 800-999-2782
http://www.apta.org

For information on accredited programs, contact
Commission on Accreditation in Physical Therapy Education
Email: accreditation@apta.org
http://www.apta.org/CAPTE

Recreational Therapists

OVERVIEW

Recreational therapists plan, organize, direct, and monitor medically approved recreation programs for patients in hospitals, clinics, and various community settings. These therapists use recreational activities to assist patients with mental, physical, or emotional disabilities to achieve the maximum possible functional independence. Recreational therapists hold approximately 24,000 jobs in the United States.

HISTORY

The field of therapy has expanded in the past few decades to include recreational therapy as a form of medical treatment. Its use grew out of the realization that soldiers suffering from battle fatigue, shock, and emotional trauma respond positively to organized recreation and activity programs.

As a result, therapy for people in nursing homes, hospitals, mental institutions, and adult care facilities is no longer limited to physical therapy. Experiments have shown that recovery is aided by recreational activities such as sports, music, art, gardening, dance, drama, field trips, and other pastimes. Elderly people are more healthy and alert when their days are filled with activities, field trips, and social get-togethers. People with disabilities can gain greater self-confidence and awareness of their own abilities when they get involved with sports, crafts, and other activities. People recovering from drug or alcohol addiction can reaffirm their self-worth through directed hobbies, clubs, and sports. The recreational therapist is a health professional who

QUICK FACTS

School Subjects
Biology
Psychology

Personal Skills
Helping/teaching
Technical/scientific

Work Environment
Indoors and outdoors
Primarily one location

Minimum Education Level
Bachelor's degree

Salary Range
$20,880 to $34,990 to $65,000

Certification or Licensing
Required by certain states

Outlook
More slowly than the average

DOT
076

GOE
14.06.01

NOC
3144

O*NET-SOC
29-1125.00

organizes these types of activities and helps patients take an active role in their own recovery.

THE JOB

Recreational therapists work with people with mental, physical, or emotional disabilities. They are professionals who employ leisure activities as a form of treatment, much as other health practitioners use surgery, drugs, nutrition, exercise, or psychotherapy. Recreational therapists strive to minimize patients' symptoms, restore function, and improve their physical, mental, and emotional well-being. Enhancing the patient's ability to take part in everyday life is the primary goal of recreational therapy; interesting and rewarding activities are the means for working toward that goal.

Recreational therapists work in a number of different settings, including mental hospitals, psychiatric day hospitals, community mental health centers, nursing homes, adult day care programs, residential facilities for the mentally disabled, school systems, and prisons. They can work as individual staff members, as independent consultants, or as part of a larger therapeutic team. They may get personally involved with patients or direct the work of assistants and support staff.

The recreational therapist first confers with the doctors, psychiatrists, social workers, physical therapists, and other professionals on staff to coordinate their efforts in treatment. The recreational therapist needs to understand the nature of the patient's ailment, current physical and mental capacities, emotional state, and prospects for recovery. The patient's family and friends are also consulted to find out the patient's interests and hobbies. With this information, the recreational therapist then plans an agenda of activities for that person.

To enrich the lives of people in hospitals and other institutions, recreational therapists use imagination and skill in organizing beneficial activities. Sports, games, arts and crafts, movie screenings, field trips, hobby clubs, and dramatics are only a few examples of activities that can enrich the lives of patients. Some therapists specialize in certain areas. *Dance/movement therapists* plan and conduct dance and body movement exercises to improve patients' physical and mental well-being. *Art therapists* work with patients in various art methods, such as drawing, painting, and ceramics, as part of their therapeutic and recovery programs. Therapists may also work with pets and other animals, such as horses. *Music therapists* design programs for patients that can involve solo or group singing, playing in bands, rhythmic and other creative activities, listening to music, or attending concerts. Even flowers and gardening can prove beneficial to patients, as is proved by the work of *horticultural therapists*. When the treatment team feels that regular employment would help certain patients, the *industrial therapist* arranges a productive job for the patient in an actual work environment, one that will have the greatest therapeutic value based on the patient's needs and abilities. *Orientation therapists* for the blind work with people who have recently lost their sight, helping them to readjust to daily living and independence through training and exercise. All of these professional therapists plan their programs to meet the needs and capabilities of patients. They also carefully monitor and record each patient's progress and report it to the other members of the medical team.

As part of their jobs, recreational therapists need to understand their patients and set goals for their progress accordingly. A patient having trouble socializing, for example, may have an interest in playing chess but be overwhelmed by the prospect of actually playing, since that involves interaction with another person. A therapist would proceed slowly, first letting the patient observe a number of games and then assigning a therapeutic assistant to serve as a chess partner for weeks or even months, as long as it takes for the patient to gain enough confidence to seek out other patients for chess partners. The therapist makes a note of the patient's response, modifies the therapy program accordingly, and lets other professionals know of the results. If a patient responds more enthusiastically to the program, works more cooperatively with others, or becomes more disruptive, the therapist must note these reactions and periodically reevaluate the patient's activity program.

Responsibilities and elements of the job can vary, depending on the setting in which the recreational therapist works. In nursing homes, the therapist often groups residents according to common or shared interests and ability levels and then plans field trips, parties, entertainment, and other group activities. The therapist documents residents' responses to the activities and continually searches for ways of heightening residents' enjoyment of recreational and leisure activities, not just in the facility but in the surrounding community as well. Because nursing home residents are likely to remain in the facility for months or even years, the activities program makes a big difference in the quality of their lives. Without the stimulation of interesting events to look forward to and participate in, the daily routine of a nursing home can become monotonous and depressing, and some residents are apt to deteriorate both mentally and physically. In some nursing homes, recreational therapists direct the activities program. In others, activities coordinators plan and carry out the program under the part-time supervision of a consultant who is either a recreational or occupational therapist.

A recreational therapist play-acts medical procedures with a boy who has leukemia. *(John Griffin, The Image Works)*

The therapist in a community center might work in a day-care program for the elderly or in a program for mentally disabled adults operated by a county recreation department. No matter what the disability, recreational therapists in community settings face the added logistical challenge of arranging transportation and escort services, if necessary, for prospective participants. Coordinating transportation is less of a problem in hospitals and nursing homes, where the patients all live under one roof. Developing therapeutic recreation programs in community settings requires a large measure of organizational ability, flexibility, and ingenuity.

REQUIREMENTS

High School

You can prepare for a career as a recreational therapist by taking your high school's college preparatory program. Naturally, this should include science classes, such as biology and chemistry, as well as mathematics and history classes. You can begin to gain an understanding of human behavior by taking psychology and sociology classes. For exposure to a variety of recreation specialties, take physical education, art, music, and drama classes. Verbal and written communication skills are essential for this work, so take English and speech classes. This job will require you to write reports, so computer science skills are also essential.

Postsecondary Training

Approximately 150 recreational therapy programs, which offer degrees ranging from the associate to the doctoral level, are currently available in the United States. While associate degrees in recreational therapy exist, such a degree will allow you only to work at the paraprofessional level. To be eligible for an entry-level professional position as a recreational therapist, you will need a bachelor's degree. Acceptable majors are recreational therapy, therapeutic recreation, and recreation with a concentration in therapeutic recreation. A typical four-year bachelor's degree program includes courses in both natural science (such as biology, behavioral science, and human anatomy) and social science (such as psychology and sociology). Courses more specific to the profession include programming for special populations; rehabilitative techniques including self-help skills, mobility, signing for the deaf, and orientation for the blind; medical equipment; current treatment approaches; legal issues; and professional ethics. In addition, you will need to complete a supervised internship or field placement lasting a minimum of 480 hours.

Continuing education is increasingly becoming a requirement for professionals in this field. Many therapists attend conferences and seminars and take additional university courses. A number of professional organizations (for example, the National Therapeutic Recreation Society, the American Therapeutic Recreation Association, and the American Alliance for Health, Physical Education, Recreation and Dance) offer continuing education opportunities. Those with degrees in related fields can enter the profession by earning master's degrees in therapeutic recreation. Advanced degrees are recommended for those seeking advancement to supervisory, administrative, and teaching positions. These requirements will become more strict as more professionals enter the field.

Certification or Licensing

A number of states regulate the profession of therapeutic recreation. Licensing is required in some states; professional certification (or eligibility for certification) is required in others; titling is regulated in some states and at some facilities. In other states, many hospitals and other employers require recreational therapists to be certified. Certification is recommended for recreational therapists as a way to show professional accomplishment. It is available through the National Council for Therapeutic Recreation Certification. To receive certification you must meet eligibility requirements, including education and experience, as well as pass an exam. You are then given the title of certified therapeutic recreation specialist. Because of the variety of certification and licensing requirements, you must check with both your state and your employer for specific information on your situation.

Other Requirements

To be a successful recreational therapist, you must enjoy and be enthusiastic about the activities in which you involve your clients. You will also need patience and a positive attitude. Since this is people-oriented work, therapists must be able to relate to many different people in a variety of settings. They must be able to deal assertively and politely with other health care workers, such as doctors and nurses, as well as with the clients themselves and their families. In addition, successful therapists must be creative and have strong communication skills in order to develop and explain activities to patients.

EXPLORING

If you are interested in recreational therapy, you can find part-time or summer work as a sports coach or referee, park supervisor, or camp counselor. Volunteer work in a nursing home, hospital, or care facility for disabled adults is also a good way to learn about the daily realities of institutional living. These types of facilities are always looking for volunteers to work with and visit patients. Working with people with physical, mental, or emotional disabilities can be stressful, and volunteer work is a good way for you to test whether you can handle this kind of stress.

EMPLOYERS

Recreational therapists hold approximately 24,000 jobs, according to the U.S. Department of Labor. About 60 percent of these jobs are in nursing care facilities and hospitals. Other employers include residential facilities, adult day care centers, and substance abuse centers, and some therapists are self-employed. Employment opportunities also exist in long-term rehabilitation, home health care, correctional facilities, psychiatric facilities, and transitional programs.

STARTING OUT

There are many methods for finding out about available jobs in recreational therapy. A good place to start is the job notices and want ads printed in the local newspapers, bulletins from state park and recreation societies, and publications of the professional associations previously mentioned. State employment agencies and human service departments will know of job openings in state hospitals. College career services offices might also be able to put new recreational therapy graduates in touch with prospective employers. Internship programs are sometimes available, offering good opportunities to find potential full-time jobs.

Recent graduates should also make appointments to meet potential employers personally. Most colleges and universities offer career counseling services. Most employers will make themselves available to discuss their programs and the possibility of hiring extra staff. They may also guide new graduates to other institutions currently hiring therapists. Joining professional associations, both state and national, and attending conferences are good ways to meet potential employers and colleagues.

ADVANCEMENT

Newly graduated recreational therapists generally begin as *staff therapists*. Advancement is chiefly to supervisory or administrative positions, usually after some years of experience and continuing education. Some therapists teach, conduct research, or do consulting work on a contract basis; a graduate degree is essential for moving into these areas.

Many therapists continue their education but prefer to continue working with patients. For variety, they may choose to work with new groups of people or get a job in a new setting, such as moving from a retirement home to a facility for the disabled. Some may also move to a related field, such as special education, or sales positions involving products and services related to recreational therapy.

EARNINGS

Salaries of recreational therapists vary according to educational background, experience, certification, and region of the country. Recreational therapists had median earnings of $34,990 in 2006, according to the U.S. Department of Labor. The lowest paid 10 percent earned less than $20,880 a year, while the highest paid 10 percent earned more than $55,530 annually. Employment setting is also an important factor in determining salary. Recreational therapists employed by nursing care facilities earned mean incomes of $32,010, while those employed by general medical and surgical hospitals earned $40,030. Those in management positions command higher salaries. Supervisors report top salaries of $50,000 per year; administrators reported maximum earnings of $65,000 annually; and some consultants and educators reported even higher earnings.

Therapists employed at hospitals, clinics, and other facilities generally enjoy a full benefits package, including health insurance and vacation, holiday, and sick pay. Consultants and self-employed therapists must provide their own benefits.

WORK ENVIRONMENT

Working conditions vary, but recreational therapists generally work in a ward, a specially equipped activity room, or at a nursing home. In a community setting, recreational therapists may interview subjects and plan activities in an office, but they might work in a gymnasium, swimming pool, playground, or outdoors on a nature walk when leading activities. Therapists may also work on horse ranches, farms, and other outdoor facilities catering to people with disabilities.

The job may be physically tiring because therapists are often on their feet all day and may have to lift and carry equipment. Recreational therapists generally work a standard 40-hour week, although weekend and evening hours may be required. Supervisors may have to work overtime, depending on their workload.

OUTLOOK

The U.S. Department of Labor predicts that employment for recreational therapists will grow more slowly than the average for all occupations through 2014. Employment in nursing homes will grow slightly faster than in other areas. Fast employment growth is expected in assisted living, outpatient physical and psychiatric rehabilitation, and services for people with disabilities. Increased life expectancies for the elderly and for people with developmental disabilities such as Down Syndrome will create opportunities for recreational therapists. The incidence of alcohol and drug dependency problems is also growing, creating a demand for qualified therapists to work in short-term alcohol and drug abuse clinics.

Most openings for recreational therapists will be in health care and assisted living facilities because of the increasing numbers and greater longevity of the elderly. There is also greater public pressure to regulate and improve the quality of life in retirement centers, which may mean more jobs and increased scrutiny of recreational therapists.

Growth in hospital jobs is not expected to be great. Many of the new jobs created will be in hospital-based adult day care programs or in units offering short-term mental health services. Because of economic and social factors, no growth is expected in public mental hospitals. Many of the programs and services formerly offered there are being shifted to community residential facilities for those with disabilities. Community programs for special populations are expected to expand significantly.

FOR MORE INFORMATION

For career information and resources, contact
American Association for Physical Activity and Recreation
1900 Association Drive
Reston, VA 20191-1598
Tel: 800-213-7193
http://www.aahperd.org/aapar

For career information, a list of colleges and universities that offer training, and job listings, contact
American Therapeutic Recreation Association
1414 Prince Street, Suite 204
Alexandria, VA 22314-2896
Tel: 703-683-9420
Email: atra@atra-tr.org
http://www.atra-tr.org

For information on certification, contact
National Council for Therapeutic Recreation Certification
Seven Elmwood Drive
New City, NY 10956-5136
Tel: 845-639-1439
Email: nctrc@nctrc.org
http://www.nctrc.org

For career information, visit the NTRS under "Branches and Sections" on the Web site of the National Recreation and Park Association.
National Therapeutic Recreation Society (NTRS)
22377 Belmont Ridge Road
Ashburn, VA 20148-4501
Tel: 703-858-0784
Email: ntrsnrpa@nrpa.org
http://www.nrpa.org

Visit this Web site to find out about jobs, activities, schools, and other information related to the field.
Therapeutic Recreation Directory
http://www.recreationtherapy.com

Rehabilitation Counselors

OVERVIEW

Rehabilitation counselors provide counseling and guidance services to people with disabilities to help them resolve life problems and to train for and locate work that is suitable to their physical and mental abilities, interests, and aptitudes. There are approximately 131,000 rehabilitation counselors working in the United States.

HISTORY

Today it is generally accepted that people with disabilities can and should have the opportunity to become as fully independent as possible in all aspects of life, from school to work and social activities. In response to the needs of disabled war veterans, Congress passed the first Vocational Rehabilitation Act in 1920. The act set in place the Vocational Rehabilitation Program, a federal-state program that provides for the delivery of rehabilitation services, including counseling, to eligible people with disabilities.

The profession of rehabilitation counseling has its roots in the Rehabilitation Act, which allowed for funds to train personnel. What was at first a job title developed into a fully recognized profession as it became evident that the delivery of effective rehabilitation services required highly trained specialists. Early efforts for providing rehabilitation counseling and other services were often directed especially toward the nation's veterans. In 1930, the Veterans Administration was created to supply support services to veterans and their families, and in 1989, the U.S. Department of Veterans Affairs was created as the 14th cabinet department in the U.S. government.

QUICK FACTS

School Subjects
Psychology
Sociology

Personal Skills
Helping/teaching
Technical/scientific

Work Environment
Primarily indoors
Primarily one location

Minimum Education Level
Bachelor's degree

Salary Range
$19,260 to $29,200 to $53,170+

Certification or Licensing
Recommended

Outlook
Faster than the average

DOT
045

GOE
12.02.02

NOC
4153

O*NET-SOC
21-1015.00

The passage of the Americans with Disabilities Act in 1990 recognized the rights and needs of people with disabilities and developed federal regulations and guidelines aimed at eliminating discrimination and other barriers preventing people with disabilities from participating fully in school, workplace, and public life. Many state and federal programs have since been created to aid people with disabilities.

THE JOB

Rehabilitation counselors work with people with disabilities to identify barriers to medical, psychological, personal, social, and vocational functioning and to develop a plan of action to remove or reduce those barriers.

Clients are referred to rehabilitation programs from many sources. Sometimes they seek help on their own initiative; sometimes their families bring them in. They may be referred by a physician, hospital, or social worker, or they may be sent by employment agencies, schools, or accident commissions. A former employer may seek help for the individual.

The counselor's first step is to determine the nature and extent of the disability and evaluate how that disability interferes with work and other life functions. This determination is made from medical and psychological reports as well as from family history, educational background, work experience, and other evaluative information.

The next step is to determine a vocational direction and plan of services to overcome the handicaps to employment or independent living.

The rehabilitation counselor coordinates a comprehensive evaluation of a client's physical functioning abilities and vocational interests, aptitudes, and skills. This information is used to develop vocational or independent-living goals for the client and the services necessary to reach those goals. Services that the rehabilitation counselor may coordinate or provide include physical and mental restoration, academic or vocational training, vocational counseling, job analysis, job modification or reasonable accommodation, and job placement. Limited financial assistance in the form of maintenance or transportation assistance may also be provided.

The counselor's relationship with the client may be as brief as a week or as long as several years, depending on the nature of the problem and the needs of the client.

REQUIREMENTS

High School

To prepare for a career in rehabilitation counseling, take your high school's college prep curriculum. These classes should include several years of mathematics and science, such as biology and chemistry. To begin to gain an understanding of people and societies, take history, psychology, and sociology classes. English classes are important to take because you will need excellent communication skills for this work. Some of your professional responsibilities will include documenting your work and doing research to provide your clients with helpful information; to do these things you will undoubtedly be working with computers. Therefore, you should take computer science classes so that you are skilled in using them. In addition, you may want to consider taking speech and a foreign language, both of which will enhance your communication skills.

Postsecondary Training
Although some positions are available for people with a bachelor's degree in rehabilitation counseling, these positions are usually as aides and offer limited advancement opportunities. Most employers require the rehabilitation counselors working for them to hold master's degrees. Before receiving your master's, you will need to complete a bachelor's degree with a major in behavioral sciences, social sciences, or a related field. Another option is to complete an undergraduate degree in rehabilitation counseling. Keep in mind, however, that even if you get an undergraduate degree in rehabilitation, you will still need to attend a graduate program to qualify for most counselor positions. No matter which undergraduate program you decide on, you should concentrate on courses in sociology, psychology, physiology, history, and statistics as well as courses in English and communications. Several universities now offer courses in various aspects of physical therapy and special education training. Courses in sign language, speech therapy, and a foreign language are also beneficial.

Both the Council for Accreditation of Counseling and Related Educational Programs and the Council on Rehabilitation Education accredit graduate counseling programs. A typical master's program in rehabilitation counseling usually lasts two years. Studies include courses in medical aspects of disability, psychosocial aspects of disability, testing techniques, statistics, personality theory, personality development, abnormal psychology, techniques of counseling, occupational information, and vocational training and job placement. A supervised internship is also an important aspect of a program.

Certification or Licensing
The regulation of counselors is required in 48 states and the District of Columbia. This regulation may be in the form of credentialing, registry, certification, or licensure. Regulations, however, vary by state and sometimes by employer. For example, an employer may require certification even if the state does not. You will need to check

Vocational Rehabilitation and Education Program Helps Injured Veterans Live More Productive Lives

Jeanne Patterson, president of the National Rehabilitation Counseling Association and professor and director of the Rehabilitation Counseling Program at the University of North Florida, explains how the Vocational Rehabilitation and Education Program of the U.S. Department of Veterans Affairs plays a key role in improving the lives of injured veterans:

> Veterans who acquire disabilities while in the service are often eligible for the Vocational Rehabilitation and Education Program (VR&E). Similarly, some veterans leave the military and their conditions may worsen over the years. Thus, rehabilitation counselors who work with veterans may provide assistance to a 25-year-old who has been diagnosed with multiple sclerosis while in the military, or a 50-year-old veteran of the Vietnam War, or a 28-year-old who received injuries in Iraq.
>
> The primary focus of the VR&E program is helping veterans acquire jobs; however, despite improvements in medical treatment many veterans are unable to return to work. This is true of Iraq war veterans who have survived very serious injuries. Some injuries are so severe that these veterans are unable to be retrained or re-enter the workforce. For some of these veterans, the VR&E

with your state's licensing board as well as your employer for specific information about your circumstances.

Across the country, many employers now require their rehabilitation counselors to be certified by the Commission on Rehabilitation Counselor Certification (CRCC). The purpose of certification is to provide assurance that professionals engaged in rehabilitation counseling meet set standards and maintain those standards through continuing education. To become certified, counselors must pass an extensive written examination to demonstrate their knowledge of rehabilitation counseling. The CRCC requires the master's degree as the minimum educational level for certification. Applicants who meet these certification requirements receive the designation of certified rehabilitation counselor.

Most state government rehabilitation agencies require future counselors to meet state civil service and merit system regulations. The applicant must take a competitive written examination and may also be interviewed and evaluated by a special board.

Independent Living Program can help them live more independently. These veterans can elect to have an Independent Living (IL) Assessment. If they will benefit from IL services, an Individualized Independent Living Plan may be developed. Since the plan is individualized, no two veterans receive the same services. For example, a veteran with post-traumatic stress disorder (PTSD) who sustained gunshot wounds to the leg and face may have difficulty remembering to take prescribed medications, getting in and out of a shower or chair, and putting on shoes. An independent living plan may include the provision of a shower chair, handheld shower, a grab bar alongside the shower, a medication reminder watch, a lift chair, and a referral to a PTSD group. Case management services are usually provided to veterans who have an IL plan to ensure that any devices or services help the veteran become more independent and provide measurable results. In this example, the veteran may no longer need the assistance of his wife or children in getting out of the chair or taking a shower and can independently put on his shoes with the use of elastic shoelaces and a long-handled shoe horn. The decrease in the number of missed medications provides a measurable indication of the benefit of a medication reminder watch.

Many of the services provided by the Veterans Administration are available to nonveterans through each state's Department of Vocational Rehabilitation, as well as Independent Living Programs within the state.

Other Requirements

The most important personal attribute required for rehabilitation counseling is the ability to get along well with other people. Rehabilitation counselors work with many different kinds of clients and must be able to see situations and problems from their client's point of view. They must be both patient and persistent. Rehabilitation may be a slow process with many delays and setbacks. The counselor must maintain a calm, positive manner even when no progress is made.

EXPLORING

To explore a career in which you work with people with disabilities, you should look for opportunities to volunteer or work in this field. One possibility is to be a counselor at a children's camp for disabled youngsters. You can also volunteer with a local vocational rehabilitation agency or a facility such as the Easter Seal Society or Goodwill. Other possibilities include reading for the blind or leading a hobby or craft class at an adult day care center. And don't forget volunteer opportunities at a local hospital or nursing home. Even if your only responsibility is to escort people to the X-ray department or talk to patients to cheer them up, you will gain valuable experience interacting with people who are facing challenging situations.

EMPLOYERS

Approximately 131,000 rehabilitation counselors are employed in the United States. Counselors work in a variety of settings. About three-quarters of rehabilitation counselors work for state agencies; some also work for local and federal agencies. Employment opportunities are available in rehabilitation centers, mental health agencies, developmental disability agencies, sheltered workshops, training institutions, and special schools. Other rehabilitation counselors teach at colleges and universities.

STARTING OUT

School career services offices are the best places for the new graduate to begin the career search. In addition, the National Rehabilitation Counseling Association and the American Rehabilitation Counseling Association (a division of the American Counseling Association) are sources for employment information. The new counselor may also apply directly to agencies for available positions. State and local vocational rehabilitation agencies employ about 10,000 rehabilitation counselors. The Department of Veterans Affairs employs counselors to assist with the rehabilitation of veterans with disabilities. Many rehabilitation counselors are employed by private for-profit or nonprofit rehabilitation programs and facilities. Others are employed in industry, schools, hospitals, and other settings, while others are self-employed.

ADVANCEMENT

The rehabilitation counselor usually receives regular salary increases after gaining experience in the job. He or she may move from relatively easy cases to increasingly challenging ones. Counselors may advance into such positions as administrator or supervisor after several years of counseling experience. It is also possible to find related counseling and teaching positions, which may represent an advancement in other fields.

EARNINGS

Salaries for rehabilitation counselors vary widely according to state, community, employer, and the counselor's experience. The U.S. Department of Labor reports that median annual earnings of rehabilitation counselors in 2006 were $29,200. Salaries ranged from less than $19,260 to more than $53,170.

Rehabilitation counselors employed by the federal government generally start at the GS-9 or GS-11 level. In 2007, basic GS-9 salary was $38,224. Those with master's degrees generally began at the GS-11 level, with a salary of $46,974 in 2007. Salaries for federal government workers vary according to the region of the country in which they work. Those working in areas with a higher cost of living receive additional locality pay.

Counselors employed by government and private agencies and institutions generally receive health insurance, pension plans, and other benefits, including vacation, sick, and holiday pay. Self-employed counselors must provide their own benefits.

WORK ENVIRONMENT

Rehabilitation counselors work approximately 40 hours each week and do not usually have to work during evenings or weekends. They work both in the office and in the field. Depending on the type of training required, lab space and workout or therapy rooms may be available. Rehabilitation counselors must usually keep detailed accounts of their progress with clients and write reports. They may spend many hours traveling about the community to visit employed clients, prospective employers, trainees, or training programs.

OUTLOOK

The passage of the Americans with Disabilities Act of 1990 increased the demand for rehabilitation counselors. As more local, state, and federal programs are initiated that are designed to assist people with disabilities and as private institutions and companies seek to comply with this new legislation, job prospects are promising. Budget pressures may serve to limit the number of new rehabilitation counselors to be hired by government agencies; however, the overall outlook remains excellent.

The U.S. Department of Labor predicts that employment for all counselors will grow faster than average for all occupations through 2014. Some of this growth can be attributed to the advances in medical technology that are saving more lives. In addition, more employers are offering employee assistance programs that provide mental health and alcohol and drug abuse services.

FOR MORE INFORMATION

For general information on careers in rehabilitation counseling, contact
American Rehabilitation Counseling Association
5999 Stevenson Avenue
Alexandria, VA 22304-3300
Tel: 800-347-6647
http://www.arcaweb.org

For information on certification, contact
Commission on Rehabilitation Counselor Certification
300 North Martingale Road, Suite 460
Schaumburg, IL 60173-2088
Tel: 847-944-1325
Email: info@crccertification.com
http://www.crccertification.com

For listings of CORE-approved programs as well as other information, contact
Council on Rehabilitation Education (CORE)
300 North Martingale Road, Suite 460
Schaumburg, IL 60173-2088
Tel: 847-944-1345
http://www.core-rehab.org

To learn about government legislation, visit the NRA's Web site.
National Rehabilitation Association (NRA)
633 South Washington Street
Alexandria, VA 22314-4109
Tel: 703-836-0850
Email: info@nationalrehab.org
http://www.nationalrehab.org

*The NRCA is a division of the National Rehabilitation Association.
For news on legislation, employment, and other information, contact*
National Rehabilitation Counseling Association (NRCA)
PO Box 4480
Manassas, VA 20108-4480
Tel: 703-361-2077
Email: NRCAOFFICE@aol.com
http://nrca-net.org

For information on a variety of resources, contact
National Clearinghouse of Rehabilitation Training Materials
Utah State University
6524 Old Main Hill
Logan, UT 84322-6524
Tel: 866-821-5355
Email: ncrtm@cc.usu.edu
http://ncrtm.org

INTERVIEW

Dr. Jeanne Patterson is the president of the National Rehabilitation Counseling Association and professor and director of the Rehabilitation Counseling Program at the University of North Florida in Jacksonville, Florida. She has worked in rehabilitation counseling for more than 30 years. Jeanne discussed her experiences and the field with the editors of Careers in Focus: Therapists.

Q. What made you want to become a rehabilitation counselor?

A. I grew up knowing I wanted to work with people, but I thought my college majors and career options were limited to more well-known fields such as nursing or psychology. A friend told me about rehabilitation counseling, which focuses on working with individuals with disabilities.

My undergraduate degree in psychology was a good degree for seeking admission to a graduate program in rehabilitation counseling. Although rehabilitation counseling requires a graduate degree, there are a number of undergraduate programs in rehabilitation services or disabilities studies that provide individuals with the skills to work in various programs and agencies that provide services to people with disabilities (physical, mental, and/or emotional disabilities).

Q. What do you like most and least about your career?

A. One of the most rewarding features of being a rehabilitation counselor is having the opportunity to make a difference in the lives of individuals with disabilities and their families. I like identifying resources for people, counseling them on various career options, and perhaps most of all, serving as an advocate for people with disabilities to help them participate in all of life's activities.

Another thing I have loved most about my profession and being a rehabilitation counselor is that I can be a "generalist" or a "specialist." When I conducted vocational assessments, I was able to help individuals with a wide range of disabilities consider various career options. In conducting independent living assessments, I help individuals identify needs and the aids, opportunities, or skills to meet those needs. A rehabilitation counselor can specialize by (1) type of disability (e.g., spinal cord injury, mental health, brain injury), (2) type of service provided (e.g., assessment/vocational evaluation, case management, independent living), or (3) setting (e.g., state agency, community program, or national program). I have found rehabilitation counseling to be an extremely rewarding profession. Because I enjoy the profession so much, I went on to get my doctoral degree in order to teach rehabilitation counseling.

One of the least rewarding, but equally important, features of being a rehabilitation counselor is the importance of paperwork, regardless of the setting in which one works. The paperwork is essential to ensure that people with disabilities receive the services they need and to document that the services are provided in a timely manner. The importance of paperwork is shared by most helping professions. Most people do not enjoy the paperwork and although it is not my favorite part of the job, it is a critical element.

Q. What are the most important professional qualities for rehabilitation counselors?

A. Individuals who think they might enjoy rehabilitation counseling as a career should like working with people, love acquiring new knowledge because the field is constantly changing (e.g., new medical developments occur daily), and have good teamwork and time management skills. People from all ethnic groups and all socioeconomic groups may be born with or acquire disabilities. A rehabilitation counselor must have the skills to interact with a wide range of individuals. Many rehabilitation counselors are part of a team and must be able to work well with other team members, as well as individuals with disabilities and their families.

An individual must be a life-long learner in order to continuously acquire new knowledge about disabilities and new treatment methods. The setting in which one works requires that individuals stay abreast of new laws in the field, such as workers' compensation laws or health insurance laws.

Finally, one must have good time management skills. Many rehabilitation counselors have a large number of individuals on their caseloads. Time management is a critical element in ensuring that each individual receives services in a timely manner and that the paperwork is completed in the time allotted. Many agencies have rules that require that decisions are made and documented within a certain time frame.

Q. What advice would you give high school students who are interested in becoming rehabilitation counselors?

A. High school students who think they may be interested in a career in rehabilitation counseling can participate in service clubs that work with people with disabilities. Volunteer activities are one of the best ways for students to gain experience and assistance in determining whether rehabilitation counseling is the best profession for them. Most communities have rehabilitation hospitals or community-based organizations such as Goodwill, Easter Seals, or the ARC. Best Buddies International is a service organization that assists individuals with disabilities and some programs offered by Big Brothers Big Sisters of America focus on working with young adults with disabilities. Volunteering in a class for young adults with disabilities can provide additional insight into some of the challenges and discrimination that are faced by individuals with disabilities. Serving as a reader for a student who is blind is another way of acquiring early experience about people with disabilities. Some communities have camps for children with disabilities and appreciate assistance from volunteers. Sometimes individuals with disabilities live in nursing homes, because there is no one to provide home assistance. Volunteering at a nursing home is a good way to learn to practice listening skills and provides another opportunity to learn about disabilities.

School classes that focus on psychology, interpersonal skills, speaking, and writing also can provide a good foundation for a future in the field of rehabilitation. Rehabilitation counselors are advocates for people with disabilities. Speech classes are a way to improve one's ability to educate others about disabilities.

Q. Tell us about the National Rehabilitation Counseling Association. How important is association membership to career success in the field?

A. Belonging to a professional association is an important part of being a rehabilitation counselor. The National Rehabilitation Counseling Association (NRCA) is the largest professional association for rehabilitation counselors. In addition to the national organization, NRCA has state and local chapters. The

NRCA publishes the *Journal of Applied Rehabilitation Counseling*, which may be of interest to high school students who are interested in learning more about people with disabilities and the work of rehabilitation counselors. NRCA's National Symposium is held each year and provides a way for counselors to network, as well as gain continuing education credits. Most rehabilitation counselors become certified rehabilitation counselors, which requires them to gain 100 hours of continuing education during each five-year period. NRCA members adhere to the Code of Professional Ethics for Rehabilitation Counselors, which is critical in a profession such as rehabilitation counseling (see http://www.crccertification.com and http://nrca-net. org). Students who are interested in rehabilitation counseling can call their local division of rehabilitation services office to see if there is a local chapter or to request a job shadowing day with a counselor. Some NRCA counselors may be happy to provide mentoring for high school students who are interested in becoming rehabilitation counselors.

Q. What is the future employment outlook for rehabilitation counselors?

A. The employment outlook for rehabilitation counselors is excellent. The field of rehabilitation is facing an "aging out" of employees, and most agencies are experiencing high retirement rates. The community-based programs, as well as state divisions of vocational rehabilitation, and the Department of Veterans Affairs all need rehabilitation counselors. High school students who think they may be interested in rehabilitation counseling can also read about the different types of counselors in the U.S. Department of Labor's *Occupational Outlook Handbook* (http://www.bls.gov/oco/ocos067.htm).

If you think you would like to work with people, rehabilitation counseling may be a wonderful profession for you to consider. People with disabilities often face barriers, and rehabilitation counselors help individuals overcome those barriers. As the Americans with Disabilities Act states, "The Nation's proper goals regarding individuals with disabilities are to assure equality of opportunity, full participation, independent living, and economic self-sufficiency for such individuals." Rehabilitation counselors perform an important role in ensuring full participation for people with disabilities.

Respiratory Therapists and Technicians

OVERVIEW

Respiratory therapists, also known as respiratory care practitioners, evaluate, treat, and care for patients with deficiencies or abnormalities of the cardiopulmonary (heart/lung) system by either providing temporary relief from chronic ailments or administering emergency care where life is threatened. They supervise other respiratory care workers in their area of treatment. *Respiratory technicians* have many of the same responsibilities as therapists; however, technicians do not supervise other respiratory care workers.

Working under a physician's direction, these workers set up and operate respirators, mechanical ventilators, and other devices. They monitor the functioning of the equipment and the patients' response to the therapy and maintain the patients' charts. They also assist patients with breathing exercises, and inspect, test, and order repairs for respiratory therapy equipment. They may demonstrate procedures to trainees and other health care personnel. Approximately 118,000 respiratory therapists and 19,000 respiratory technicians are employed in the United States.

HISTORY

In normal respiration, the chest muscles and the diaphragm (a muscular disk that separates the chest and abdominal cavities) draw in air by expanding the chest volume. When this automatic response is impaired because of illness or injury, artificial means must be applied to keep the patient breathing and to prevent brain damage or death. Respiratory problems can result from many conditions. For example, with bronchial asthma, the bronchial tubes are narrowed by spasmodic contractions, and they produce an excessive amount of mucus. Emphysema is a disease in which the lungs lose their elasticity. Diseases of the central nervous system and drug poisoning may result in paralysis, which could lead to suffocation. Emergency conditions such as heart failure, stroke, drowning, or shock also interfere with the normal breathing process.

Respirators, or ventilators, are mechanical devices that enable patients with cardiorespiratory problems to breathe. The iron lung was designed in 1937 by Philip Drinker and Louise A. Shaw, of the Harvard School of Public Health in Boston, primarily to treat people with polio. It was a cylindrical machine that enclosed the patient's entire body, except the head. This type of respirator is still in use today. The newer ventilators, however, are small dome-shaped breastplates that wrap around the patient's chest and allow more freedom of motion. Other sophisticated, complex equipment to aid patients with breathing difficulties includes mechanical ventilators, apparatuses that administer therapeutic gas, environmental control systems, and aerosol generators.

Respiratory therapists and technicians and their assistants are the workers who operate this equipment and administer care and life support to patients suffering from respiratory problems.

THE JOB

Respiratory therapists and technicians treat patients with various cardiorespiratory problems. They may provide care that affords temporary relief from chronic illnesses such as asthma or emphysema, or they may administer life-support treatment to victims of heart failure, stroke, drowning, or shock. These specialists often mean the difference between life and death in cases involving acute respiratory conditions, as may result from head injuries or drug poisoning. Adults who stop breathing for longer than three to five minutes rarely survive without serious brain damage, and an absence of respiratory activity for more than nine minutes almost always results in death. Respiratory therapists carry out their duties under a physician's direction and supervision. Technicians typically work under the supervision of a respiratory therapist and physician, following specific instructions. Therapists and technicians set up and operate special devices to treat patients who need temporary or emergency relief from breathing difficulties. The equipment may include respirators, positive-pressure breathing machines, or environmental control systems. Aerosol inhalants are administered to confine medication to the lungs. Respiratory therapists often treat patients who have undergone surgery because anesthesia depresses normal respiration, thus the patients need some support to restore their full breathing capability and to prevent respiratory illnesses.

In evaluating patients, therapists test the capacity of the lungs and analyze the oxygen and carbon dioxide concentration and potential of hydrogen (pH), a measure of the acidity or alkalinity level of the blood. To measure lung capacity, therapists have patients breathe into an instrument that measures the volume and flow of air during inhalation and exhalation. By comparing the reading with the norm for the patient's age, height, weight, and gender, respiratory therapists can determine whether lung deficiencies exist. To analyze oxygen, carbon dioxide, and pH levels, therapists draw an arterial blood sample, place it in a blood gas analyzer, and relay the results to a physician.

Respiratory therapists watch equipment gauges and maintain prescribed volumes of oxygen or other inhalants. Besides monitoring the equipment to be sure it is operating properly, they observe the patient's physiological response to the therapy and consult with physicians in case of any adverse reactions. They also record pertinent identification and therapy information on each patient's chart and keep records of the cost of materials and the charges to the patients.

Therapists instruct patients and their families on how to use respiratory equipment at home, and they may demonstrate respiratory therapy procedures to trainees and other health care personnel. Their responsibilities include inspecting and testing equipment. If it is faulty, they either make minor repairs themselves or order major repairs.

Respiratory therapy workers include therapists, technicians, and assistants. Differences between respiratory therapists' duties and those of other respiratory care workers include supervising technicians and assistants, teaching new staff, and bearing primary responsibility for the care given in their areas. At times the respiratory therapist may need to work independently and make clinical judgments on the type of care to be given to a patient. Although technicians can perform many of the same activities as a therapist (for example, monitoring equipment, checking patient responses, and giving medicine), they do not make independent decisions about what type of care to give. *Respiratory assistants* clean, sterilize, store, and generally take care of the equipment but have very little contact with patients.

REQUIREMENTS
High School
To prepare for a career in this field while you are still in high school, take health and science classes, including biology, chemistry, and physics. Mathematics and statistics classes will also be useful to

you since much of this work involves using numbers and making calculations. Take computer science courses to become familiar with using technical and complex equipment and to become familiar with programs you can use to document your work. Since some of your responsibilities may include working directly with patients to teach them therapies, take English classes to improve your communication skills. Studying a foreign language may also be useful.

Postsecondary Training

Formal training is necessary for entry to this field. Training is offered at the postsecondary level by hospitals, medical schools, colleges and universities, trade schools, vocational-technical institutes, and the armed forces. The Committee on Accreditation for Respiratory Care (CoARC) has accredited more than 350 programs nationwide. A listing of these programs is available on CoARC's Web site, http://www.coarc.com. To be eligible for a respiratory therapy program, you must have graduated from high school.

Accredited respiratory therapy programs combine class work with clinical work. Programs vary in length, depending on the degree awarded. A certificate program generally takes one year to complete, an associate's degree usually takes two years, and a bachelor's degree program typically takes four years. In addition, it is important to note that some advanced-level programs will prepare you for becoming a registered respiratory therapist (RRT), while entry-level programs will prepare you for becoming a certified respiratory therapist (CRT). RRT-prepared graduates will be eligible for jobs as respiratory therapists once they have been certified. CRT-prepared graduates, on the other hand, are only eligible for jobs as respiratory technicians after certification. The areas of study for both therapists and technicians cover human anatomy and physiology, chemistry, physics, microbiology, and mathematics. Technical studies include courses such as patient evaluation, respiratory care pharmacology, pulmonary diseases, and care procedures.

There are no standard hiring requirements for assistants. Department heads in charge of hiring set the standards and may require only a high school diploma.

Certification and Licensing

The National Board for Respiratory Care (NBRC) offers voluntary certification to graduates of CoARC-accredited programs. The certifications, as previously mentioned, are registered respiratory therapist (RRT) and certified respiratory therapist (CRT). You must have at least an associate's degree to be eligible to take the CRT exam.

Anyone desiring certification must take the CRT exam first. After successfully completing this exam, those who are eligible can take the RRT exam. CRTs who meet further education and experience requirements can qualify for the RRT credential.

Certification is highly recommended because most employers require this credential. Those who are designated CRT or are eligible to take the exam are qualified for technician jobs that are entry-level or generalist positions. Employers usually require those with supervisory positions or those in intensive care specialties to have the RRT (or RRT eligibility). The NBRC also offers certification in neonatal/pediatric respiratory care for therapists who have the CRT credential plus one year of clinical experience in neonatal/pediatric respiratory care (or have the RRT credential) and pass an examination.

All states (except Alaska and Hawaii) require respiratory therapists to obtain a license. Requirements vary, so you will need to check with your state's regulatory board for specific information. The NBRC Web site provides helpful contact information for state licensure agencies at http://www.nbrc.org/StateLicAgencies.htm.

Other Requirements

If you plan to work as a respiratory therapist, you must enjoy working with people. You must be sensitive to your patients' physical and psychological needs because you will be dealing with people who may be in pain or who may be frightened. The work of this occupational group is of great significance. Respiratory therapists are often responsible for the lives and well-being of people already in critical condition. You must pay strict attention to detail, be able to follow instructions and work as part of a team, and remain calm in emergencies. Mechanical ability and manual dexterity are necessary to operate much of the respiratory equipment.

EXPLORING

Those considering advanced study may obtain a list of accredited educational programs in respiratory therapy by visiting the American Association for Respiratory Care's Web site, http://www.aarc.org/education. Formal training in this field is available in hospitals, vocational-technical institutes, private trade schools, and other noncollegiate settings as well. Local hospitals can provide information on training opportunities. School vocational counselors may be sources of additional information about educational matters and may be able to set up interviews with or lectures by a respiratory therapy practitioner from a local hospital.

Hospitals are excellent places to obtain part-time and summer employment. They have a continuing need for helpers in many departments. Even though the work may not be directly related to respiratory therapy, you will gain knowledge of the operation of a hospital and may be in a position to get acquainted with respiratory therapists and observe them as they carry out their duties. If part-time or temporary work is not available, you may wish to volunteer your services.

EMPLOYERS

Approximately 118,000 respiratory therapists and 19,000 respiratory technicians are employed in the United States. More than four out of five respiratory therapy jobs are in hospital departments of respiratory care, anesthesiology, or pulmonary medicine. The rest are employed by oxygen equipment rental companies, ambulance services, nursing homes, home health agencies, and physicians' offices. Many respiratory therapists (13 percent, as opposed to 5 percent in other occupations) hold a second job.

STARTING OUT

Graduates of CoARC-accredited respiratory therapy training programs may use their school's career services offices to help them find jobs. Otherwise, they may apply directly to the individual local health care facilities.

High school graduates may apply directly to local hospitals for jobs as respiratory therapy assistants. If your goal is to become a therapist or technician, however, you will need to enroll in a formal respiratory therapy educational program.

ADVANCEMENT

Many respiratory therapists start out as assistants or technicians. With appropriate training courses and experience, they advance to the therapist level. Respiratory therapists with sufficient experience may be promoted to assistant chief or chief therapist. With graduate education, they may be qualified to teach respiratory therapy at the college level or move into administrative positions such as director.

EARNINGS

Respiratory therapists earned a median salary of $47,420 in 2006, according to the U.S. Department of Labor. The lowest paid 10 percent earned less than $35,200, and the highest paid 10 percent earned more than $64,190. Median annual earnings of respiratory therapy technicians were $39,120 in 2006. Salaries ranged from less than $25,940 to more than $56,220.

Hospital workers receive benefits that include health insurance, paid vacations and sick leave, and pension plans. Some institutions provide additional benefits, such as uniforms and parking, and offer free courses or tuition reimbursement for job-related courses.

WORK ENVIRONMENT

Respiratory therapists generally work in extremely clean, quiet surroundings. They usually work 40 hours a week, which may include nights and weekends because hospitals are in operation 24 hours a day, seven days a week. The work requires long hours of standing and may be very stressful during emergencies.

A possible hazard is that the inhalants these employees work with are highly flammable. The danger of fire is minimized, however, if the workers test equipment regularly and are strict about taking safety precautions. As do workers in many other health occupations, respiratory therapists run a risk of catching infectious diseases. Careful adherence to proper procedures minimizes the risk.

OUTLOOK

Employment for respiratory therapists is expected to grow at a faster than average rate through 2014, despite the fact that efforts to control rising health care costs has reduced the number of job opportunities in hospitals.

The increasing demand for therapists is the result of several factors. The fields of neonatal care and gerontology are growing, and there are continuing advances in treatments for victims of heart attacks and accidents and for premature babies.

Employment opportunities for respiratory therapists and technicians should be very favorable in the rapidly growing field of home health care, although this area accounts for only a small number of respiratory therapy jobs. In addition to jobs in home health agencies and hospital-based home health programs, there should be numerous openings for respiratory therapists in equipment rental companies and in firms that provide respiratory care on a contract basis.

FOR MORE INFORMATION

For information on scholarships, continuing education, job listings, and careers in respiratory therapy, contact

American Association for Respiratory Care
9425 North MacArthur Boulevard, Suite 100

Irving, TX 75063-4706
Tel: 972-243-2272
Email: info@aarc.org
http://www.aarc.org

For more information on allied health care careers as well as a list-ing of accredited programs, contact
**Commission on Accreditation of Allied Health Education
    Programs**
1361 Park Street
Clearwater, FL 33756-6039
Tel: 727-210-2350
Email: mail@caahep.org
http://www.caahep.org

For a list of CoARC-accredited training programs, contact
Committee on Accreditation for Respiratory Care (CoARC)
1248 Harwood Road
Bedford, TX 76021-4244
Tel: 817-283-2835
http://www.coarc.com

For information on licensing and certification, contact
National Board for Respiratory Care
18000 West 105th Street
Olathe, KS 66061-7543
Tel: 913-895-4900
http://www.nbrc.org

Speech-Language Pathologists and Audiologists

OVERVIEW

Speech-language pathologists and *audiologists* help people who have speech and hearing defects. They identify the problem and use tests to further evaluate it. Speech-language pathologists try to improve the speech and language skills of clients with communications disorders. Audiologists perform tests to measure the hearing ability of clients, who may range in age from the very young to the very old. Since it is not uncommon for clients to require assistance for both speech and hearing, pathologists and audiologists may frequently work together to help clients. Some professionals decide to combine these jobs into one, working as speech-language pathologists and audiologists. Audiologists and speech-language pathologists may work for school systems, in private practice, and at clinics and other medical facilities. Other employment possibilities for these professionals include teaching at universities, and conducting research on what causes certain speech and hearing defects. There are approximately 106,000 speech-language pathologists and audiologists employed in the United States.

HISTORY

The diagnosis and treatment of speech and hearing defects is a new part of medical science. In the past, physicians

QUICK FACTS

(continued)

O*NET-SOC
29-1127.00, 29-1121.00

were not able to help patients with these types of problems because there was usually nothing visibly wrong, and little was known about how speech and hearing were related. Until the middle of the 19th century, medical researchers did not know whether speech defects were caused by lack of hearing, or whether the patient was the victim of two separate ailments. And even if they could figure out why something was wrong, doctors still could not communicate with the patient.

Alexander Graham Bell, the inventor of the telephone, provided some of the answers. His grandfather taught elocution (the art of public speaking), and Bell grew up interested in the problems of speech and hearing. It became his profession, and by 1871 Bell was lecturing to a class of teachers of deaf people at Boston University. Soon afterward, Bell opened his own school, where he experimented with the idea of making speech visible to his pupils. If he could make them see the movements made by different human tones, they could speak by learning to produce similar vibrations. Bell's efforts not only helped deaf people of his day, but also led directly to the invention of the telephone in 1876. Probably the most famous deaf person was Helen Keller, whose teacher, Anne Sullivan, applied Bell's discoveries to help Keller overcome her blindness and deafness.

THE JOB

Even though the two professions seem to blend together at times, speech-language pathology and audiology are very different from one another. However, because both speech and hearing are related to one another, a person competent in one discipline must have familiarity with the other.

The duties performed by speech-language pathologists and audiologists differ depending on education, experience, and place of employment. Most speech-language pathologists provide direct clinical services to individuals and independently develop and carry out treatment programs. In medical facilities, they may work with physicians, social workers, psychologists, and other therapists to develop and execute treatment plans. In a school environment, they develop individual or group programs, counsel parents, and sometimes help teachers with classroom activities.

Clients of speech-language pathologists include people who cannot make speech sounds, or cannot make them clearly; those with speech rhythm and fluency problems such as stuttering; people with voice quality problems, such as inappropriate pitch or harsh voice; those with problems understanding and producing language; and those with cognitive communication impairments, such as attention, memory, and problem-solving disorders. Speech-language pathologists may also work with people who have oral motor problems that cause eating and swallowing difficulties. Clients' problems may be congenital, developmental, or acquired, and caused by hearing loss, brain injury or deterioration, cerebral palsy, stroke, cleft palate, voice pathology, mental retardation, or emotional problems.

Speech-language pathologists conduct written and oral tests and use special instruments to analyze and diagnose the nature and extent of impairment. They develop an individualized plan of care, which may include automated devices and sign language. They teach clients how to make sounds, improve their voices, or increase their language skills to communicate more effectively. Speech-language pathologists help clients develop, or recover, reliable communication skills.

People who have hearing, balance, and related problems consult audiologists, who use audiometers and other testing devices to discover the nature and extent of hearing loss. Audiologists interpret these results and may coordinate them with medical, educational, and psychological information to make a diagnosis and determine a course of treatment.

Hearing disorders can result from trauma at birth, viral infections, genetic disorders, or exposure to loud noise. Treatment may include examining and cleaning the ear canal, fitting and dispensing a hearing aid or other device, and audiologic rehabilitation (including auditory training or instruction in speech or lip reading). Audiologists provide fitting and tuning of cochlear implants and help those with implants adjust to the implant amplification systems. They also test noise levels in workplaces and conduct hearing protection programs in industrial settings, as well as in schools and communities.

Audiologists provide direct clinical services to clients and sometimes develop and implement individual treatment programs. In some environments, however, they work as members of professional teams in planning and implementing treatment plans.

In a research environment, speech pathologists and audiologists investigate communicative disorders and their causes and ways to improve clinical services. Those teaching in colleges and universities instruct students on the principles and bases of communication, communication disorders, and clinical techniques used in speech and hearing.

Speech-language pathologists and audiologists keep records on the initial evaluation, progress, and discharge of clients to identify problems and track progress. They counsel individuals and their families on how to cope with the stress and misunderstanding that often accompany communication disorders.

REQUIREMENTS

High School

Since a college degree is a must for practicing this profession, make sure your high school classes are geared toward preparing you for higher education. Health and science classes, including biology, are very important. Mathematics classes and English classes will help you develop the math, research, and writing skills you will need in college. Because speech-language pathologists and audiologists work so intensely with language, you may also find it beneficial to study a foreign language, paying special attention to how you learn to make sounds and remember words. Speech classes will also improve your awareness of sounds and language as well as improve your speaking and listening skills.

Postsecondary Training

Most states require a master's degree in speech-language pathology or audiology for a beginning job in either profession. Speech-language pathologists are required to be licensed in 47 states if they work in a health care setting, and 11 states require the same degree to practice in a public school. Typical majors for those going into this field include communication sciences and disorders, speech and hearing, or education. Regardless of your career goal (speech-language pathologist or audiologist), your undergraduate course work should include classes in anatomy, biology, physiology, physics, and other related areas, such as linguistics, semantics, and phonetics. It is also helpful to have some exposure to child psychology. Accredited graduate programs in speech-language pathology are available from approximately 240 colleges and universities.

To be eligible for certification, which most employers and states require, you must have at least a master's degree from a program accredited by the accreditation council of the American Speech-Language-Hearing Association (ASHA). Currently there are more than 400 programs in speech-language pathology and/or audiology; however, not all of these programs are accredited. It is in your best interest to contact the ASHA for a listing of accredited programs before you decide on a graduate school to attend. Accredited graduate programs in speech-language pathology are available from approximately 240 colleges and universities. According to the ASHA, as of 2012, audiologists will have to earn a doctorate in order to be certified.

Some schools offer graduate degrees only in speech-language pathology or graduate degrees only in audiology. A number of schools offer degrees in both fields. Graduate-level course work in audiology includes such studies as hearing and language disorders, normal auditory and speech-language development, balance, and audiology instrumentation. Graduate-level work for those in speech-language pathology includes studies in evaluating and treating speech and language disorders, stuttering, pronunciation, and voice modulation. Students of both disciplines are required to complete supervised clinical fieldwork or practicum.

If you plan to go into research, teaching, or administration, you will need to complete a doctorate degree.

Certification or Licensing

To work as a speech pathologist or audiologist in a public school, you will be required to be a certified teacher and you must meet special state requirements if treating children with disabilities. Almost all states regulate audiology and/or speech-language pathology through licensure or title registration, and all but six of those require continuing education for license renewal. In order to become licensed, you must have completed an advanced degree in the field (generally a master's degree, but a doctorate is becoming the new standard for audiologists), pass a standardized test, and complete 300 to 375 hours of supervised clinical experience and nine months of postgraduate professional clinical experience. Some states permit audiologists to dispense hearing aids under an audiology license. Specific education and experience requirements, type of regulation, and title use vary by state.

Many states base their licensing laws on ASHA certification. ASHA offers speech-language pathologists the certificate of clinical competence in speech-language pathology and audiologists the certificate of clinical competence in audiology. To be eligible for these certifications, you must meet certain education requirements, such as the supervised clinical fieldwork experience, and have completed a postgraduate clinical fellowship. The fellowship must be no less than 36 weeks of full-time professional employment or its part-time equivalent. You must then pass an examination in the area in which you want certification.

Other Requirements

Naturally, speech-language pathologists and audiologists should have strong communication skills. Note, though, that this means more than being able to speak clearly. You must be able to explain diagnostic test results and treatment plans in an easily understood

A speech-language therapist teaches sign language to a deaf girl.
(Elizabeth Crews, The Image Works)

way for a variety of clients who are already experiencing problems. As a speech-language pathologist and audiologist, you should enjoy working with people, both your clients and other professionals who may be involved in the client's treatment. In addition, you need patience and compassion. A client's progress may be slow, and you should be supportive and encouraging during these times.

EXPLORING

Although the specialized nature of this work makes it difficult for you to get an informal introduction to either profession, there are opportunities to be found. Official training must begin at the college or university level, but it is possible for you to volunteer in clinics and hospitals. As a prospective speech-language pathologist and audiologist, you may also find it helpful to learn sign language or volunteer your time in speech, language, and hearing centers.

EMPLOYERS

There are approximately 96,000 speech-language pathologists and 10,000 audiologists employed in the United States. About one-half of speech-language pathologists are employed in education, from elementary school to the university level. More than half of all audiologists work in physicians' offices and medical facilities. Other professionals in this field work in state and local governments, hearing aid stores (audiologists), and scientific research facilities. A small but growing number of speech-language pathologists and audiologists are in private practice, generally working with patients referred to them by physicians and other health practitioners.

Some speech-language pathologists and audiologists contract to provide services in schools, hospitals, or nursing homes, or work as consultants to industry.

STARTING OUT

If you want to work in the public school systems, your college career services office can help you with interviewing skills. Professors sometimes know of job openings and may even post these openings on a centrally located bulletin board. It may be possible to find employment by contacting a hospital or rehabilitation center. To work in colleges and universities as a specialist in the classroom, clinic, or research center, it is almost mandatory to be working on a graduate degree. Many scholarships, fellowships, and grants for assistants are available in colleges and universities giving courses in speech-language pathology and audiology. Most of these and other assistance programs are offered at the graduate level. The U.S. Rehabilitation Services Administration, the Children's Bureau, the U.S. Department of Education, and the National Institutes of Health allocate funds for teaching and training grants to colleges and universities with graduate study programs. In addition, the Department of Veterans Affairs provides stipends (a fixed allowance) for predoctoral work.

ADVANCEMENT

Advancement in speech-language pathology and audiology is based chiefly on education. Individuals who have completed graduate study will have the best opportunities to enter research and administrative areas, supervising other speech-language pathologists or audiologists either in developmental work or in public school systems.

EARNINGS

The U.S. Department of Labor reports that in 2006 speech-language pathologists earned a median annual salary of $57,710. Salaries ranged from to less than $37,970 to more than $90,400. Also in 2006, audiologists earned a median annual salary of $57,120. The lowest paid 10 percent of these workers earned less than $38,370, while the highest paid 10 percent earned $89,160 or more per year.

Geographic location and type of facility are important salary variables. Almost all employment situations provide fringe benefits such as paid vacations, sick leave, and retirement programs.

WORK ENVIRONMENT

Most speech-language pathologists and audiologists work 40 hours a week at a desk or table in clean comfortable surroundings. Speech-language pathologists and audiologists who focus on research, however, may work longer hours. The job is not physically demanding but does require attention to detail and intense concentration. The emotional needs of clients and their families may be demanding.

OUTLOOK

Population growth, lengthening life spans, and increased public awareness of the problems associated with communicative disorders indicate a highly favorable employment outlook for well-qualified personnel. The U.S. Department of Labor predicts that employment for speech-language pathologists and audiologists will grow about as fast as the average for all occupations through 2014. Much of this growth depends on economic factors, further budget cutbacks by health care providers and third-party payers, and legal mandates requiring services for people with disabilities.

Nearly half of the new jobs emerging through the end of the decade are expected to be in speech and hearing clinics, physicians' offices, and outpatient care facilities. Speech-language pathologists and audiologists will be needed in these places, for example, to carry out the increasing number of rehabilitation programs for stroke victims and patients with head injuries.

Substantial job growth will continue to occur in elementary and secondary schools because of the Education for All Handicapped Children Act of 1975 (which was renamed the Individuals with Disabilities Education Act and amended in 1990, 1997, and 2004). This law guarantees special education and related services to minors with disabilities.

Many new jobs will be created in hospitals, nursing homes, rehabilitation centers, and home health agencies; most of these openings will probably be filled by private practitioners employed on a contract basis. Opportunities for speech-language pathologists and audiologists in private practice should increase in the future. There should be a greater demand for consultant audiologists in the area of industrial and environmental noise as manufacturing and other companies develop and carry out noise-control programs.

FOR MORE INFORMATION

The American Auditory Society is concerned with hearing disorders, how to prevent them, and the rehabilitation of individuals with hearing and balance dysfunction.

American Auditory Society
352 Sundial Ridge Circle
Dammeron Valley, UT 84783-5196
Tel: 435-574-0062
http://www.amauditorysoc.org

This professional, scientific, and credentialing association offers information about communication disorders and career and membership information.

American Speech-Language-Hearing Association
2200 Research Boulevard
Rockville, MD 20850-3289
Tel: 800-638-8255
Email: actioncenter@asha.org
http://www.asha.org

This association is for undergraduate and graduate students studying human communication. For information on accredited training programs, news related to the field, and to find out about regional chapters, contact

National Student Speech Language Hearing Association
2200 Research Boulevard, No. 450
Rockville, MD 20850
Tel: 301-296-8705
Email: nsslha@asha.org
http://www.nsslha.org

Index

Entries in **boldface** indicate main articles.

A

AAHPERD. *See* American Alliance for Health, Physical Education, Recreation and Dance

AAP. *See* American Academy of Pediatrics

AAPB. *See* Association for Applied Psychophysiology and Biofeedback

AATA. *See* American Art Therapy Association

Academy for Certification of Vision Rehabilitation and Education Professionals 132, 136

Accreditation Council for Occupational Therapy Education. *See* American Occupational Therapy Association, Accreditation Council for Occupational Therapy Education

ACHE. *See* American Council of Hypnotist Examiners

ACOTE. *See* American Occupational Therapy Association, Accreditation Council for Occupational Therapy Education

activity therapists. *See* child life specialists

acupressure. *See* shiatsu and acupressure

acupuncture 90, 111

Addams, Jane 130

ADEC. *See* Association for Death Education and Counseling

AER. *See* Association for Education and Rehabilitation of the Blind and Visually Impaired

African culture 6

AHTA. *See* American Horticultural Therapy Association

aides. *See* occupational therapy aides

AKTA. *See* American Kinesiotherapy Association

alpha rhythms 30, 32

alternative therapy practitioners. *See specific careers*

American Academy of Kinesiology and Physical Education 84

American Academy of Pediatrics (AAP) 45, 46

American Alliance for Health, Physical Education, Recreation and Dance (AAHPERD) 84, 161

American Association for Marriage and Family Therapy 22, 102

American Association for Music Therapy 100

American Association for Physical Activity and Recreation 165

American Association for Respiratory Care 185–186

American Association of People with Disabilities 135, 136

American Association of Professional Hypnotherapists 75

American Art Therapy Association (AATA) 21, 24, 25

American Auditory Society 195

American Board of Physical Therapy Specialties 142

American College of Sports Medicine 81

American Community Gardening Association 65

American Counseling Association 22, 49, 52, 102, 172

American Council of Hypnotist Examiners (ACHE) 71, 74, 75

American Horticultural Therapy Association (AHTA) 62, 63, 64, 65

American Kinesiotherapy Association (AKTA) 81, 82, 83, 84–85, 86

American Massage Therapy Association (AMTA) 16, 91, 94, 96–97

American Music Therapy Association (AMTA)
-approved programs 101
beginnings of music therapy discipline 99
certification 102
contact information 105
earnings data 104
founding of 100
job openings list 103
job outlook 105
journals 102
Member Sourcebook 104

American Occupational Therapy Association (AOTA)
Accreditation Council for Occupational Therapy Education (ACOTE) 118, 125
career information 126
contact information 122, 128
employment bulletins 120, 127
postsecondary training recommendations 117, 119

American Pacific University 76

American Physical Therapy Association (APTA)
certification 142
contact information 145, 155
founding of 139, 148
job postings 143
postsecondary training 151

American Psychological Association 22, 25, 102